Incantations
Embodied

Incantations Embodied

Rituals for Empowerment, Reclamation, and Resistance

Kimberly Rodriguez

SPIRIT BOUND
press.

Spirit Bound Press is dedicated to preserving authenticity in the books we publish and honoring the voices of the communities we embrace. We proudly reveal our communities' sacred stories, wisdom, medicine, and magic, actively reshaping the prevailing narrative towards inclusivity, diversity, and empowerment in the literary world.

To honor our authors' voices and protect their intellectual property, any reproduction of this book (except for short quotations used for reviews) without permission is strictly prohibited. For usage requests, please contact us at rights@spiritboundpress.com.

Published by Spirit Bound Press with Row House Publishing

Library of Congress Cataloging-in-Publication Data Available Upon Request

ISBN 978-1-955905-55-8 (TP)
ISBN 978-1-955905-38-1 (eBook)

Printed in the United States
Distributed by Simon & Schuster

First edition
10 9 8 7 6 5 4 3 2 1

To those who have ever felt they do not belong on the lands that were taken from their ancestors; to the ancestors who persevered despite the obstacles they faced; to all the grandmothers who preserved the rituals they watched their own mothers craft; to my parents, who showed me that resilience is my relative; to Madre Tierra, who has showered me with healing and peace; to my sisters and brother, who have uplifted me with cheers and prayers; to my husband, whose kindness and love have allowed me to seek kindness and love toward myself—it is through all of you that the words in this book exist; it is because of you that I write this book.

Tlazohcamati.

Contents

conjuro

Introducción
(Introduction)

If you do not let them know who you are, they will make up tales of you. They will assume and shape-shift you into a creature of their own making. They will paint you with pale tones of Eurocentric beauty standards. They will press in every curve, every belly roll that rebels against our fatphobic culture. They will overwork you until your spine cracks, because here, in this society, you must carry the scar to prove you are worthy. They will insist that you be obedient and do not cuss. But justified anger gets a kick from saying "fuck" or "shit." They will don muted colors on you, even though your spirit is vibrant in color like the lands of your ancestors. They will tell you to slow dance, even though your feet swing up to every *cumbia* song. They will smear you with religion and tell you God is found only in holy cathedrals, even though you see God in everything. They will clamp the shackles of purity on you when they don't understand what true purity means, thinking virginity equals virtue. They will take away the embroidery, the braids, the huaraches, the Nahuatl from your tongue, and tell you that you can live here, but only if you forget who you are. They will tell you to stay, but never let you live.

If you do not let them know who you are, they will make up tales of you.
If you do not let them know who you are, they will make up tales of you.

"If you do not let them know who you are, they will make up tales of you, *mija*," my *amá* (mother) once said to me. "Do you wish to walk distorted, unrecognized, a stranger to yourself?" She whispered in Spanish as she looked in the mirror, searching for a glimpse of the person she once was. As her sharp eyes met her reflection, a little smirk lifted the corner of her mouth, showing me she still held on to a golden strand of herself. Amá did what she had to do so we could survive, often with limited choices. But her reflection in the mirror told me she did not wish a similar fate for me.

"Hay poder en existir cuando vives con
propósito y a propósito, mija."

(There is power in existing when you live
with purpose and on purpose, darling.)

AMÁ

Amá grabbed my hand and stared at me for what felt like eternity. In that moment of gazing at each other, our spirits collided, unraveling centuries of obedience, expectations, and obligations, and weaving together resilience and liberation. We didn't speak much after she told me those words. We never spoke much back then. Not before I found my own words, not before I became an entire incantation, embodied and raw, not before my tongue found spells and my body a home. I learned from my mother that words don't always come in sounds or verbal frequencies, at least they didn't for her. She was never taught to invoke the full power of her voice. Amá showed me that words may come in silent agreements, gestures, and nods, in *presentimientos* (feelings), in held hands, and silent stares. Silent and spoken words hold power. Yet, it us up to us whether we receive them or let them pass by.

It is through dancing and moving that I tell my story.
It is through singing and chanting that I heal my story.

EMBODIED

The Power of Words

Throughout generations, our words have been silenced. Our spoken and written words have been restricted to appease a colonizer mentality. This system of oppression harms many of us, especially Black and Brown, Indigenous People, Disabled People, LGBTQIA2S+ People and countless more who fall under the label, "other." Since birth, we've been told how we must speak and what words we must never speak. We've been tormented into quieting ourselves so we can be safe. The privilege to speak freely, loudly, and honestly was taken from us, just as our land was. For this reason, finding our words, finding a language that speaks to our spirit is challenging but crucial if our stories are to survive.

"Chingate, huey!" (Go fuck yourself, idiot!) This was the phrase that made me fall in love with the power of words. I was twelve years old, living with my family in San Diego, California, the land of the Indigenous Kumeyaay People—the land where I was born. Amá had sent me on the ten-minute walk to the local grocery store to get ingredients for a salsa she was making. I skipped into the store, greeted Toño, the owner of Tres Amigos Supermercado, and bought my ingredients. On my way back home, a black Honda with tinted windows slowed as it approached me. A voice from the window of the car said, "Hey! Need a ride, *chiquita*?" I looked up to see a pair of predatory eyes moving from my face down to my growing preteen body. His filthy mouth nearly ruined the word *chiquita* (little girl) for me. In my culture, *chiquita* is a term of endearment for young kids or for sweet talking a loved one. For this man, it meant something different.

The words just flew out of my twelve-year-old mouth. *"Chingate, huey!"* (Go fuck yourself, idiot!)

I know, right? A twelve-year-old knowing such words . . . I had no idea my tongue possessed so much fire until that moment. I just wanted him to stop bothering me. The catcaller scrunched up his eyebrows, opened his mouth, but nothing came out. Defeated, he rolled up his window and drove away.

In that moment, I had summoned the fury of my ancestors with my words. I'm not the kind of person who would normally tell someone to go and fuck themselves, but I am proud I stood up for myself, and I know my ancestors are, too. I could have stayed silent, embarrassed by my growing body, my head cast down the entire walk home. Instead, I shot words from my mouth like flaming arrows to ward off evil. I only use that kind of strong language when I need to protect myself. When I do, I fire it off to show *quien muerde mas fuerte* (who bites the strongest).

Words can awaken the *brujx/e* in us. (The word *brujx/e* is a gender-nonconforming term reworked from the Spanish "*bruja/o*," witch or sorcerer. It's pronounced *brew-hex*) Your inner *brujx/e* can summon forgotten powers and ancient wisdom. In our modern, colonized society, we are pressured to alter our appearance, our customs, and even our dialect. We're taught we cannot say "no," and that "yes" buys us approval. We're taught to say "sorry," when we have no reason to apologize. Sometimes, shame makes us choke down our words. But words have a way of rising from the deep caves within. In this book, I'll show you how to harness the liberating incantations on these pages and embody the forces around and within you so you can become who you were always meant to be. When we reclaim our words and awaken our *brujx/e* powers, without shame or resistance, no one will ever be able to silence us or keep us down again.

I am but a simple prayer, cracked open and pouring.
A spell that has manifested.
The stream that becomes the ocean.
The candle that melts into a burning fire.
The feather that harnesses the air.

The pebble that creates a road.
The spirit living between bones and purpose.

Incantations Are Our Liberation

The incantations in this book are concoctions of carefully crafted words or prayers to be used as magical spells of empowerment. We speak, hum, scream, or feel an incantation to provide an intentional outcome. They reflect parts of ourselves back to us. They invoke the deep energy of our spirit that is longing for expression. They trigger memories and invigorate our bodies. Memory is only a speck in the vast landscape of who we are, but the body—the body is made from ancient elements. It holds the wisdom of the universe. As we navigate life, the simplest of incantations moving through our bodies can inspire, motivate, liberate, and guide us.

I call upon the forces of my ancestors. May their sacred
wisdom and resilience guide me as I break barriers in this
moment when others wish for me to be small and silent.

Incantations awaken our magic. With the power of words, we become conjurers, bringing our wildest dreams to life. These are not merely affirmations. The incantations in this book were crafted from the wisdom of my ancestors, the ancient knowledge of nature, and the fierceness of my spirit. I invite you, dear friend, to harness the incantations that speak to your spirit, protect and love like your ancestors, awaken your body, and connect you to all that is or ever was.

I sing to prove nothing and to surrender everything.
I chant to find a home for the words that forgot they are my own.

A Warning

The incantations in this book are powerful and should be used with profound care and respect. With each incantation, you are summoning ancient wisdom to come to your aid and help you release that which does not belong to you. My hope is that your life will grow and change as you integrate these practices into your life. You might notice reduced stress, more beauty, less drama, and higher self-worth.

Incantations are not about false positivity. I acknowledge our human right to feel anger, sadness, frustration, stress, or even boredom. There is a difference between letting our shadow emotions dictate our lives and fully feeling them, allowing them to move through us so we can release them. Toxic positivity has no place between these pages, nor in our sacred practices. It is important to be honest with yourself as you explore the incantations in this book. Find what resonates with you, modify as necessary to fit your unique human experiences and needs, and leave the rest.

Our Embodiment Garden

Our body is our garden. Our skin carries ancient memories, just like the crust of the earth. Salt water surrounds the cells in our bodies, carrying the life-nurturing magic of the oceans. We hold fire in our bellies, capable of breaking down nutrients to keep us strong and alive. The wind in our lungs is the same as the air that lifts eagles' wings as they soar in the sky. When we embody incantations, we are planting seeds that strengthen, nurture, and enlighten every cell in our beings. Embodiment helps us connect to one another and our surroundings. (More on this later.)

I am both rational and spiritual
But never more rational than spiritual
My mind and body understand
But my spirit always knows

Anyone Can Embody These Incantations

No matter your background, race, religion, age, or how you identify, this book is here for all. It is my belief that no matter who we are or where we are from, we have all been harmed by the colonial capitalist ghost that I call Fodonga (a Spanish word used to describe someone who is gross, filthy, dirty, grimy, or lazy). Fodonga has been taunting us with its screams, deceit, and archaic rules for many decades. It is time we liberate ourselves from Fodonga's grip.

If you've ever been silenced or ignored, if you've been forced into shame or are feeling disconnected from yourself and others, this book is for you, dear friend. It's an invitation to befriend yourself. To those who were taught that *"calladita/o/x te ves mas bonita/o/x"* (you look prettier by being silent), let these offerings break the chains around your voice. The practices, exercises, and rituals in this book will remove the bonds from your wings so you may fly again. Between these pages, we will banish Fodonga, no matter how scary it may seem.

Maybe it's not about being brave.
Maybe it's about being afraid and doing it anyway,
Because we deserve to see what could be.

Travel with me through portals of self-discovery, self-awareness, creativity, reclamation, and the healing of generational trauma. It is my wish for you that on this path, you'll reunite with your own forgotten and lost words so you can reclaim your purpose and magic. Our words have the ability to dismantle systems that have polluted our mind, body, and spirit. It is time for you, dear friend, to reclaim your words.

How to Use This Book

Incantations Embodied is offered in four parts. Each part has its own chapters, which I call "offerings." These offerings will take you on specific pathways of healing, growth, resistance, and self-compassion. On the first page of each offering, you will find an illustration that is meant to act as a portal into your quest. Take a moment to meditate on each illustration, pay attention to the emotions that come up for you, notice any intuitive feelings rising within you as you invite the illustration into your being. Allow yourself to be an open channel, letting the image flow through you and simmer in your bones, your spirit, and your heart. To increase accessibility, I have included descriptions for each illustration. You can find these descriptions in the appendix at the end of the book.

Beneath the illustration at the beginning of each offering will be two incantations: a long one and a shortened one (one that is easier to memorize or write on a note where you can see it every day). Each incantation is specifically written for that offering. Let the words infuse your spirit. Let them bring up what needs to come up. Explore what needs to be explored. Acknowledge that each incantation is a spell that is meant to break open the shell that traps you so you can liberate your spirit.

Throughout this process, I welcome you to alter, rewrite, or do what you please with any incantations offered in this book. They will adapt to the spirit of the person receiving them. You may change each incantation to make it suitable for your own needs. You will want to keep an embodiment journal to write or draw your own spells, observations, and responses to the journal prompts throughout this book. I have left room for you to draw and write within these pages, but you may find you need more space, so a journal is a good companion.

Each offering contains an embodiment exercise, a practice, and a ritual. They contain the potential for profound healing, connection, and empowerment. As with the incantations, these exercises, practices, and rituals may be modified to fit individuals with all abilities, experiences, and lineages. They are guides to encourage you to start your own loving practice within yourself.

At the end of each offering, you will see another illustration. Unlike the initial illustration, which is a portal to the journey ahead, the ending illustration is a reflection of what you've just read. It is the visual of the energy you've embodied after absorbing the offering. Take a moment to meditate upon this illustration, feel its energy, and welcome it into your body and spirit. Journal about your experience.

Every word offered in this book has been intentionally offered to help you fall in love with yourself and all that you are.

Loving myself is not just an act of kindness to my body.
Loving myself is a revolutionary stand against a patriarchy
that continuously tells me there is nothing to love about myself.

Your *Bruja* Guide

I am Kimberly Rodriguez, illustrator, poet, writer, child of immigrants, and *bruja* from the ancient lands of Nayarit, Mexico, where my ancestors and relatives, the Wixáritari, the Náayeri, and the O'odham Indigenous Peoples still live (among other Indigenous groups). My childhood was spent translating for my Spanish-speaking parents and caring for my younger siblings while our parents worked two or three jobs to provide for us. Words and art literally saved me. And they continue to teach me. I am an Indigenous Chicana whose parents migrated from the lands of their ancestors and were called "immigrants" by those who stole sacred land. It is through my healing and reconnection to my lineage that I am here to guide you in reclaiming the parts of you that were stolen. I come to you now as someone who has reclaimed my voice and my space to dream, explore, and express. I offer the same opportunity for you, dear friend.

I am a being who loves in two different languages, sees in two different languages, and explores in two different languages. I have lived in two different worlds my whole life. With my knowledge of love and magic across barriers, I am here now to guide you through your personal discovery *viaje* (journey) with the intent to empower you to live a life of authenticity, true to the magnificent imprint of who you are.

Note: Those who struggle with trauma should always seek out a professional who can help with coping techniques whenever possible. However, with the lack of accessibility to health insurance, I've had to figure out ways to help myself cope. I am not a psychologist, a therapist, nor a doctor. I am someone who has had to become resourceful when it comes to my physical and mental health. These exercises, practices, and rituals are not meant to replace professional therapy nor medical treatment. Rather, they are meant to be helpful companions to any treatment plan you make with professionals.

disipando

Part One

Disipando
(Dispelling)

I heal for the grandmothers who couldn't find a safe space to do so.

I heal for the mothers who didn't have the privilege of time to do so.

I heal for the fathers who were not taught the softness to do so.

I heal for the Earth who has taught me the importance of doing so.

desenredar

Offering One

Desenredar
(Unravel)

Incantation

I befriend the pain. It no longer consumes me. I remember I am a shape-shifter, a recreationalist. I know only expansiveness. I take each moment, each memory, and create strength. I allow myself to fully exist through every sensation and emotion. I do not need to hold back, overlook, or be passive. I grant myself full permission to unravel and be as I am—as my most beautiful, chaotic, and enchanting self.

Shortened Incantation

I expand beyond measure, for I do not need to shrink myself to feel loved or accepted. I see myself for who I am and wish to be, and I find beauty in me.

Desenredar,
Una Fábula

Before they are born, Madre Divina sits her Earth-bound children in her lap. She uses her long, soft fingers to comb their hair. She hums as she braids their celestial hair, singing melodies of triumph, wisdom, peace, struggle, serenity, home. Her voice forms golden strands that contain the ancient wisdom of the stars, the rhythms of Earth, its seasons and cycles, the cleansing power of the rain, the deep secrets of the ocean, and the tales trees tell one another as they whisper through their roots. Madre Divina weaves these golden strands filled with all of her wisdom, comfort, security, strength, and love into the hair of her children, forming a celestial braid.

"It's here when you need it. I'm always here with you." Madre Divina sings as her children move through the portal of life and into the world. Madre Divina knows her children may forget that they hold all the magic, wisdom, and infinite power of the universe in those celestial braids. So, she sings to them, *"Desenredar"* (Unravel).

Desenredar (Unravel)
Desenredar (Unravel)
Desenredar (Unravel)

Once upon infinity, a sacred child forgot the gifts of Madre Divina. This child was told to dress in a particular way, not too bold, not too bright. She stayed quiet to please her earthly family. But when she was alone, in a secret place in the woods, she would adorn her hair with flowers, wear bright colors, sing loudly, play in the mud, and dance with the trees. Madre Divina danced with her. The child made the wind blow as she moved through the woods with her Madre, a force at one with nature.

As this divine child grew, she learned about the expectations of the world. These expectations were like needles, draining the essence from the child. Every disapproving adult comment that pierced her when she shined too brightly, every admonishment, every judgmental glare, it all pulled her away from who she truly was, further and further. The color slowly faded from her face. Eventually, that color faded from her world. When this divine child came into the world, she knew who she was and what she had to offer. But she was forgetting.

Madre Divina wept at the child's gray appearance as her essence drained from her once rosy cheeks. She hummed to the child, making the golden strands she weaved into her hair vibrate like strings on a harp. They glowed golden around the child's head. The child was so distraught, she couldn't hear Madre Divina's song. She couldn't see the golden strands glowing above her head. Her shoulders hung low and her head sank in loneliness and disconnection.

One day, the child decided to leave Earth. She walked to the woods and lay on the ground. Her tears trickled down, offering water to the roots beneath. Again, Madre Divina hummed to her child. This time, the golden strands from before her birth vibrated with so much power, the roots in the ground pulsed, echoing Madre Divina's song:

Desenredar (Unravel)
Desenredar (Unravel)
Desenredar (Unravel)

The child felt the vibration of Earth as it harmonized with her celestial braid. The harmony resonated through her entire being until she finally heard Madre Divina's words.

Desenredar (Unravel)
Desenredar (Unravel)
Desenredar (Unravel)

The celestial braid unraveled, giving the child access to the profound love, strength, courage, and wisdom of Madre Divina, which had been with her since before she was born. She ran her fingers through the strands, remembering who she was, reconnecting with her divinity. The braid pushed like roots against Earth, propping up the child.

As the child remembered the treasures weaved into her from Madre Divina, the color came back to her face. The child looked around and saw bright, colorful flowers all around her, growing from the humming roots in the ground. Her fingers grasped the soil as she sat and watched the woods with the same wonder as before. She listened to the song of Madre Divina vibrating through the trees, the flowers, and her wild, unraveled hair.

The child danced in the woods in celebration of remembering the divine gifts from Madre Divina. Earth and the stars danced with her.

Desenredar (Unravel)
Desenredar (Unravel)
Desenredar (Unravel)

She never again forgot Madre Divina's song.

Mi *amá* (my mother) taught me how to braid my hair as soon as my fingers could coordinate with one another. She said braids are the easiest hairstyle to do in a hurry. Maybe she just didn't know what to do with my thick, cascading locks. One could weave an entire wardrobe with all the hair on the heads of my siblings and me. Braids were accessible, easy, and tamed "the *greñas,*" the name my mom gave to the tangled strands that refused to stay in place. She'd stand me in front of a mirror as her tired, rough hands slid down my long hair. My mother would grab three strands of hair and say, "*Presta atención, agarra un pedazo de mechón con este dedo y este mechón con el otro dedo, luego los enroscas debajo de cada mechón*" (Pay attention, grab a piece of hair with this finger and this hair with the other finger, then twist them under each hair). She was masterful at weaving the strands together.

As she molded my unruly locks into a thick, beautiful braid, I could hear her release a deep sigh. The sigh surrounded me in a blanket of comfort and care. I don't know if her sigh came from the simple comfort she found in braiding her children's hair, or if braiding our hair was the only sense of control she felt in her life. As Amá braided my hair, her continuous sighs felt like a thousand little releases, like something heavy was coming undone. It was as if Amá's spirit was unraveling all the heaviness she ever carried as she weaved the strands of my hair.

Growing up, I came to understand the hidden meanings of the sighs I heard from both my parents. There was a rhythm to them, like waves of the ocean. They breathed a sigh in the quiet moments in our house, another after a long day at work, another as they tucked us into bed, a soft lullaby soothing us to sleep. But not all sighs were ones of comfort and quiet. Some were of exhaustion from how hard they worked for our survival.

I come from a lineage that has persisted, despite the atrocities of colonialism. However, in that persistence, we've had to endure pain, loss, and trauma. This undercurrent of suffering has followed my ancestry throughout each generation like an unrelenting phantom we can't shake. I am a detribalized Indigenous Mexican woman whose parents migrated to a land that belonged to their ancestors before colonizer borders turned us into outcasts. As I loudly state, *"I am still here, we are still here, we have never left, we have survived,"* there is an inherited longing that aches, pulling at us all, refusing to be ignored; an ache for the belonging our ancient ancestors felt before their land was stolen.

It is my sacred responsibility to break the harmful cycles that have haunted the generations of my family. I believe that if we wish to remove the binds of a pain that have manipulated and distorted our perception of ourselves and our world, then we must unravel our generational trauma. Many families are plagued by psychological and emotional wounds that are passed down through generations.

I grew up confused about how I felt toward my mother, not knowing whether to run to her or run from her. But that's the thing about generational trauma, it will have you running in circles thinking dizziness is just a way of life. Our perception of ourselves is a reflection of how we were raised and what we grew up believing. However, I came to understand that there is a vast difference between the lies of generational trauma and the truth of who we actually are.

I know Amá never meant to be cruel in her times of frustration. Yet, at times, she spoke to us as if we had no feelings. Her tongue was like a whip, lashing us with words that cut to the bone. Perhaps this is how many undocumented parents see their children—as brick walls that do not crumble, no matter how many verbal tornados of insults and disapproval are hurled at them. We were expected to just take it, because our parents had to endure the same or worse from their parents. To them, it was a "normal" thing to do.

In between those hurtful words were sweet little moments that made my belly flutter with delight. Amá used her tired, rough hands to paint with us, to draw, sew, and play with us. Perhaps her harsh words and her playful nature were both expressions of her love for us. She wanted the best for us. She over-worked herself to provide a life for her children that was better than the one in which she grew up. Though she tried her best, I could see that she was just as hard on herself as she was on us. This cold, dark side of her that resided on the other side of her warm, bright tenderness was an ancestral shadow of verbal abuse and a generational legacy of depression; first passed down to her, and then to us.

If we want to discover who we are at the root, we must unravel ourselves from the lies our generational trauma has told us. We must detangle our spirit from the pain, the heaviness, the normalized expectations and patterns that drain our vibrant essence and suffocate us into silence. So, how do we break harmful generational cycles so they no longer dictate how we live? We must meet them with empathy.

The Embodiment of Empathy

By embodying empathy toward Amá, I was able to approach her wounds with care and understanding, rather than anger and resentment. I could see that Amá's pain was a byproduct of the environment in which she was raised and the trauma she inherited from her own mother. Amá grew up in poverty and abuse. She wasn't allowed to take up space. Talking about or processing feelings was forbidden. Instead, she was raised to know survival, servitude, and obedience. Later, Amá instilled shards of those lessons into her own children, whether she was conscious of it or not. Although she is responsible for her own actions, she was not responsible for her childhood, which influenced how she treated herself and those around her. She left her childhood with a deep well of wounds given to her by her parents, who carried wounds from their parents.

When we ignore the wounds of generational trauma, it causes a blockage. The mind, body, and spirit cannot move when there is pain blocking its natural flow. If we wish to get closer to our own truth, we must first empathize with ourselves, as well as with the people toward whom we may hold heavy feelings. Healing generational trauma does not require bypassing pain, but it does require a different perspective. I recommend finding a decolonial and culturally competent counselor/therapist to work with if possible. Ask yourself the following questions:

Who could I be without this anger?
What would my life be like without resentment?
How can I transform my pain into healing?

Some relationships are best kept at a distance, especially when they are dangerous to us. We must be able to discern for ourselves whether or not to participate in these relationships. Even with empathy, we may come to understand that not every relationship is healthy for us. In some cases, we can offer empathy while protecting ourselves and disengaging from the relationship. Empathy does not mean blind forgiveness and a million second chances.

Through my embodiment of empathy, I could see that the pain Amá carries is not who she is. Before that pain took root in her body, mind, and spirit, she was a precious child, full of potential, life, and the playfulness we glimpsed in her from time to time. In my unraveling of this generational suffering, I can now see Amá as that bright, young child full of life and hope. I can see her as her most sacred self, free of the shadows of the generational pain that weighed her down.

·

DESENREDAR EMPATHY EMBODIMENT EXERCISE

In this exercise I invite you to embody empathy for yourself or for someone who may have caused you pain.

Close your eyes and envision yourself or someone in your life standing in front of you. Imagine the fear, anger, and pain this person carries as threads that are tightly raveled around their body.

Begin by finding the loose threads of the pain and pulling each one, unraveling them from the body. With a simple pull, all the pain, fear, and anger are now becoming undone. Envision the threads unraveling from the fingertips all the way to the shoulder. Envision the threads unraveling from the toes to the thighs. With the unraveling of each body part, a soft truth is exposed underneath these layers. This truth reveals the body as a sovereign being, a growing being, a being who deserves to live in the space of love, understanding, and kindness. Continue to unravel until every layer is undone and every surface of the body underneath is free.

Once the unraveling is complete, meditate upon the being in the entirety of their truth, their sovereignty. Hold this being in its brilliant truth and playfulness with love, compassion, and empathy. Allow the new, liberated version of this being to be the one you carry with you going forward, releasing the versions of this being who caused you pain.

Slowly open your eyes. How do you feel? Write down your observations:

Unraveling the Cycle

As a young girl, I was taught to serve plates of food to the men in my family before I could even spell my name. *"Las mujeres deben atender a sus maridos"* (Women must tend to their husbands), Amá asserted as my little four-year-old hands tried their best to balance the large plates. Amá guided me to where Apá was sitting and told me to hand him his plate of food. He would take it with a big smile on his face, as if I'd just won a gold medal of approval.

Many of us were raised with gender-based expectations. For me, refusal to abide meant dishonoring my family. As a child, I was shamed and restricted into a tiny cage of expectations and obedience. As an adult, I learned that just because something in our household or society has been normalized doesn't make it right. Harmful expectations are like a baton that gets passed from one generation to the next. But we don't have to hold out our hands and take that baton.

My process of breaking generational cycles liberated me from that tiny cage of shame and restrictions. I traded obedience and servitude for bare feet and tangled hair. I stopped going to church and instead went to the forest to look for God. I grew breasts and no longer hid them in baggy clothes, because mountains are beautiful. So why hide the view? I learned to talk back, the good kind of talking back, with a voice of conviction that refuses to be belittled. I stopped resenting my mother for her harmful traits and traditions, and I also refused to claim them as my own. I stopped listening to what society told me I could be as an Indigenous Mexican woman. Instead, I focused on discovering what makes my spirit feel alive and full.

Desenredar to Free the Body

When my sister was diagnosed with depression, all I could think about was my mother . . . and my mother's mother. When I was diagnosed with a chronic disease, all I could think about was my mother . . . and her mother. When I found myself struggling to shake off the trauma of being raised in survival, all I could think was about my parents . . . and their parents. With every health diagnosis, a history stood behind it. I learned that, for generations, our family members struggled with the same diagnoses and health complications in a repetitive cycle that had gained a staggering amount of momentum. Our ancestral cycle of chronic illness and depression was so strong, almost no one escaped it, leading us all to believe it was "normal."

The more I healed my relationship with Amá, the more I perceived our similarities. Every moment of self-sabotage in my life began as an echo of her disapproving remarks bouncing off the bones in my head. I could pinpoint every erroneous belief I had about my gender identity like a map, all roads leading to my mother's legacy of normalized gender bias. I resembled Amá, in her servitude and obedience, throwing away any sense of myself that didn't match her expectations. This self-abandonment led me directly to a flimsy belief system, not rooted in the truth of who I am, but upheld by traditions of trauma. This myth of myself kept me busy, spinning in circles, until my chronic illness ground everything to a halt (more about that in Offering Eight).

My ancestors did not have the option to live free from restriction. Their culture, traditions, language, even their very existence, were all threatened by the nightmare of genocide and colonialism. But if I believe in anything, it is in them, it is in me. For I am here because they persisted. Now it is my duty to free us all from the shackles of oppression that have held us back for centuries.

Desenredar Practice: Unraveling Pain

If you can do so right now, take a moment to close your eyes and find the place in your body where you might be storing pain. Pain shows up in our body as stiffness, restricting our body from flowing with ease. When you locate this area in your body, place your hand on that area and chant this incantation:

I am not bound to the pain that lives here. I unravel every string that has carefully woven itself here. I unravel and mend my body with love.

As we unravel, every shard of destructive thought will loosen and fall away. We may never truly forget the pain we've endured. Yet, intentionally moving forward and not allowing the pain to take up space in our bodies is how we heal and grow. Dr. Clarissa Pinkola Estés, author of *Women Who Run with the Wolves: Myths and Stories of the Wild Woman Archetype*, put it beautifully when she wrote, "This kind of forgetting does not erase memory, it lays the emotion surrounding the memory to rest."[1] When we lay our suffering to rest, we are free to live a life that brings us joy.

Desenredar Journal Prompts

We are all bound by generational beliefs, gifts, traditions, and curses. What was passed down to you from your ancestors?

Which of these ancestral legacies do you wish to keep? How can they assist you on your path?

_____

_____

_____

_____

_____

Which of these ancestral beliefs, traditions, and curses do you wish to unravel and release?

_____

_____

_____

_____

_____

Now that you are choosing what you want to keep and what you want to release, how will your life be different? Envision yourself as a person who is free from the binds of generational pain, free to use the gifts passed down to you.

Write about or draw yourself as this liberated, unraveled being:

Desenredar Reflection

We all have the freedom to *desenredar* ourselves from the destruction of suffering. Rather than allowing the pain we've inherited and experienced to dictate how we live, we can open our hearts to its wisdom and choose growth. If it is empathy that liberates us from anger and resentment toward others or ourselves, it is intentionally choosing to heal that liberates our spirit.

As you heal harmful generational cycles, it may feel as if you are creating more trouble than good. Family members and friends may not understand the changes you are making for yourself and your environment. They might not see the importance of the boundaries you set. Some may be offended, feel insulted, or question your choices. You might even be questioning yourself or forget why you set out on this journey. During these times, rather than give in to the inner and outer noise, tune into your heart center and take a deep breath. In that long inhale, may you remember that your choice to break harmful generational cycles has nothing to do with others and how they view you. The changes you are cultivating in your unraveling are a departure from a system you have outgrown. You are now awakening to your potential and liberating yourself from that which restricts your magic. You are the sole creator of the life you wish to live, unbounded from the cycles that have caused you and your family harm.

Do this work with empathy, intention, and honesty. Remember that your ancestors fought for you to be here today so you could live the life of your dreams. Do not let destructive, normalized cycles keep you from accessing what is divinely and rightfully yours. May you continue to unravel and never fret over *lo que dirán* (what they may say). You are the root of a new beginning, and as you grow, your lineage will see how powerful healing can be.

I expand beyond measure, for I do not need to shrink myself to feel loved or accepted. I see myself for who I am and who I wish to be, and I find beauty in that.

I expand beyond measure, for I do not need to shrink myself to feel loved or accepted. I see myself for who I am and wish to be, and I find beauty in me.

Desenredar Ritual: A Letter of Forgiveness

This exercise has helped me process generational trauma and cultivate forgiveness. For this ritual, I invite you to write a "Letter of Forgiveness" to your generational trauma. The goal is to unravel centuries of harmful cycles that have kept you small and caged within a limited existence, so you may process and release it.

Items needed:

A piece of paper

A pen or pencil

A candle (the candle may be any color, but I prefer white).

A heat-resistant plate or pot (to hold the burning paper)

1. Create a sacred space where you feel safe and comfortable.
2. Light your candle with the intention to purge generational trauma, no matter how old the trauma is. (Fire symbolizes death, passion, destruction, and purification. After we write the letter, we are letting the fire purge our suffering and free our spirit).
3. Write a letter to your generational trauma, expressing that you forgive it for the harm it has caused you. It is perfectly okay to start the letter with "Dear Generational Trauma," or whatever words feel right to you. Write the letter as if it is intended for a person to receive it.

4. The letter does not need to be formatted any certain way. I recommend that you tune into your emotions and write whatever comes up for you, even if it's messy. Forget grammar and punctuation. Some of our wounds are ancient, before we had language. Scribble, write nonsense, or write poetry if that's in your heart. This letter is uniquely yours.

5. Be sure to focus on why you choose to forgive the trauma, rather than dwell too long on the pain it caused. What is your why? Is it to finally be at peace? Is it because you don't wish to pass the trauma down to the next generation? Is it because you are ready to move forward? Write down your reasons.

6. When you are done writing the letter, you may burn it. I prefer to let the corner of the letter catch a bit of a flame. Then I place the letter on a heat-resistant plate or pot and be present as I watch it burn all the way through. (A word of caution: Make sure you do this step in a safe place where you will not catch anything else on fire. Have a fire extinguisher handy, just in case.)

7. While watching the letter burn, turn inward. Focus all your attention on allowing yourself to be physically purified by the fire. Watch the words you wrote burn, freeing you of the burdens of generational suffering.

Read this phrase aloud to complete this ritual:

Y *así es* (and so it is).
Your ritual is complete.

reclamar

Offering Two

Reclamar
(Reclaim)

Incantation

I reflect everything that burns and everything that mends. I reflect everything that was and everything with no ends. I reflect everything that waxes and everything that wanes. I reflect everything that stays and that which carries my name.

And so, let it be that with this truth I reclaim my glory and set fire to anything that holds me back. For I seek to bring forth abundant life into everything that once lacked.

Shortened Incantation

I am the altar at which I pray. I am the Ancestor in becoming. I am the magic and all the chaos. I am purpose and destiny, voyage and arrival, reclamation and truth. I trust in myself and step into my power.

Reclamar,
Una Fábula

Long ago, our ancient ancestors wandered through the forests, valleys, fields, by the sea, and near the riverbanks. In their baskets, the ancient *brujx/e* gathered the warm light from the sun, the renewing rain from the clouds, and the secrets from the stars. From the earth, they reclaimed the red bloodroot, yellow lichens, green algae, and purple extract from the sea snail. In deep connection with the wisdom of the earth, they made medicine from plants. They collected the crystal droplets that splashed up from the river, the gems from deep in the ground, the soft hush of the ocean, the honeysuckle whisper of the breeze. They wandered the lands, reclaiming the gifts from Madre Naturaleza (Mother Nature). As the great sun sank into the pink horizon, they brought Madre Naturaleza's gifts home to their people.

Our *brujx/e* ancestors alchemized, harmonizing the hush of the ocean with the honeysuckle whisper of the breeze to make beautiful music. They reclaimed the sounds of nature, combining their melodies for rituals and sacred ceremonies. They harnessed the hush of the ocean to sing lullabies for their children. They turned the thundering hooves of the bison into rhythmic drumbeats that played as they danced in celebration around the fire. They spun the melodies of songbirds into their flutes and played songs of gratitude for the gift of being alive.

Our ancestors collaborated with Madre Naturaleza, making art from the bright, colorful plants and sea life, turning them into dyes of indigo, red, yellow, green, and all of nature's subtle shades in between. They wove the colorful threads into *huipiles, rebozos,* and *serapes*. The gifts they reclaimed from the earth were transformed into blankets to keep their babies warm. Reeds and palm leaves were crafted into baskets with the power to hold the magic of Madre Naturaleza.

The glow of the sun blessed the people with crops of maize, beans, squash, chilies, tomatoes, and other nourishing foods. Our ancestors harnessed the power of the sun to make roasted *barbacoa*. They danced in celebration around the fire and gathered near it for warmth as they shared the stories of their people. The life-giving essence of the sun pumped through their veins, granting them vitality and abundance.

Our ancient native ancestors gathered the precious stones and metals from the earth—turquoise, silver, gold, copper, fire opals, and obsidian. These treasures reclaimed from the earth were masterfully crafted into jewelry that adorned their grandmothers' wrinkled hands and hung around the necks of mothers as their babies wrapped their tiny fingers around the gems. The necklaces and rings of our ancestors were a symbol of their wealth and nobility.

Ancient *brujx/es* gathered the crystals caught from the splashes of the rivers and gems from deep in the earth. They hung them above the beds of their babies to protect them from nightmares and provide portals to their ancestors, so they could receive messages as they slept. They weaved vessels from the branches of the willow tree and the cords of plants. They reclaimed the cycle of the moon and the sun and used the rhythm of the universe to rock their babies to sleep. Even rest was sacred reclamation, comfort, and peace.

All around us are gifts from Madre Naturaleza, waiting to be reclaimed—not taken or stolen, but respectfully received in harmony with Earth, moon, and stars. To reclaim is to be in rhythm. It is to be worthy of receiving by giving back, and to have the wisdom to know what's ours. We reclaim for ourselves, our ancestors, and our children. In reclamation, there is participation in the cycles of life. We must know when to be still, when to move, when to harvest, when to fast. We must reclaim the knowing of our ancestral *brujx/es*, letting it flow through us back into the earth and forward into future generations.

Reclamation is a sacred ritual of receiving and replenishing. It requires our hearts to beat in harmony with the pulse of the land. It demands our minds be open to reception from ancient messengers. It asks us to turn our gaze to the secrets of the sun, stars, and moon. It insists on courage when what rightfully belongs to us and to nature is stolen, so that we may take back what is ours without retreating. To reclaim is to be one with all that is or ever was.

The day my great-grandmother came to visit me in a dream was the day I remembered who I am. It was the kind of remembrance where the spirit recognizes something ancient, something it thirsted for but could not find. When Great-Grandmother Socorro came to visit me, she was wearing a blue skirt that flowed just above her ankles. It was the color of blue that settles over the ocean when it's calm. She wore a white floral embroidered top, whose stitches I recognized from the pictures my *apá* (father) showed me as he told her stories. My great-grandmother's light gray curls swept across her rosy cheeks. Her face was full of life, as if she'd just done something amazing and couldn't wait to tell me all about it. She held my hands within hers and brought them up to her tiny mouth. She kissed them and said:

"Acuerdate, mija, de todo lo que eres. La memoria no viene de la mente, viene del espíritu." (Remember, *mija*, everything that you are. Memory does not come from the mind, it comes from the spirit.)

My great-grandmother gently settled my arms against my chest as she faded away like a whisper into the dark, vast universe that enveloped her.

As I awakened after Great-Grandmother Socorro's visit, everything felt different—I felt different. I never got the chance to meet Great-Grandmother Socorro while she was alive. She passed away a few years before I was born. Apá often told me stories about her. He would tell me how she cooked for the entire *vecindario* (neighborhood), where she lived, and how passing truck drivers would stop by her house for a warm plate of food before their long journey. Apá also told me stories of how Great-Grandmother Socorro *lee las cartas* (read the cards) for the local people in need of insight. Apá said she always had a serious look on her face and that she didn't laugh much, but was loving in her own way. When she came to visit me, I felt as if I had known her my entire life. That encounter taught me how to reclaim what has always been my birthright, familiar but forgotten.

Reclamar means that what was taken from us still lives within us. We reclaim it by actively living in the authenticity of our spirit. When we reclaim parts of ourselves that were stolen by a demanding society or family, we are loudly stating: "This is mine. I am this because I am imprinted on its very nature, and without me the cycle is incomplete—without me, the story does not exist." Reclaiming is the sacred right of our spirit. It is the journey on which we must embark in honor of our ancestors. Although many of us had no other choice but to assimilate and be silenced, what was stolen is never lost. It is through the process of reclaiming that we rebirth what was extinguished, that we breathe into becoming everything that was taken, including our words and stories.

Reclamar Embodiment Exercise

AN UNEXPECTED SURPRISE

We tend to live in our comfort zones, because we feel safe in the familiar. However, sometimes exploring something different can spark new abilities, strengths, and passions in us we didn't know we had. In this exercise, I invite you to do something outside of your comfort zone.

- Once a week, for an entire month, I challenge you to do something you would not normally do.
- Before you begin, think about something you've wanted to do but never felt confident or brave enough to try. Have you ever wanted to

make a friend at a bookstore but felt too shy to say hi? Maybe you wanted to wear a piece of clothing you were told wouldn't look "good" on you? Did you ever want to draw but didn't think you could learn how? Whatever you choose to try, remember that it doesn't have to be a drastic change. The point is to do something you normally wouldn't do to reclaim the parts of yourself that have been silenced or buried.

- Commit to a day of the week that you will carry out this challenge and hold yourself accountable. Do it at the same time every week for an entire month if you can.
- Every time you do this challenge, I invite you to journal about your experience. Here are some questions to address in your journal:

> How did today's challenge make me feel? Was I afraid, excited, pensive? What made me feel that way?
>
> What did this challenge teach me about myself?
>
> How did I honor myself when I completed today's challenge?
>
> How did I reclaim a part of myself as I did this challenge ? What parts did I reclaim?

The exciting part of this challenge is that you get to discover who you are. Congratulations! You are finally giving yourself the opportunity of new experiences. Have fun!

Reclaiming Our Inner Forest

Beneath the layers of who we've been told we are is an undying forest of the imprint of our spirit. It is this forest that has survived, despite ferocious fires that sought to torch it down. This imprint is the land where we meet ourselves—the part of ourselves that knows the truth of who we are. When Great-Grandmother Socorro came to visit me in a dream, I was struggling with my identity. This is an issue that many children of undocumented parents experience as we navigate two different worlds. We are torn between the rich soil of our roots and the strange customs we've been forced to adopt through assimilation. I grew up being constantly picked apart and put back together so I would fit into the restrictive roles and expectations of those around me. In the process, I almost forgot the imprint of my spirit—the words, stories, and truths of my ancestors. The struggle with my identity came from my attachment to false versions of myself, ones imposed on me by others. I had no space to freely express myself. I couldn't explore the worlds within myself I had not yet discovered. I yearned to study and create a relationship with myself that allowed me to connect to the imprint of my spirit. I'd become invested in this false self, one that pulled me away from my spirit. When Great-Grandmother Socorro said, *"Acuerdate, mija, de todo lo que eres. La memoria no viene de la mente, viene del Espíritu"* (Remember, *mija*, everything that you are. Memory does not come from the mind, it comes from the spirit), something in me shifted. I knew the truth of who I was in that moment, no matter how much my mind tried to trick me into being someone else. With my great-grandmother's words swirling in my body, mind, and spirit, I awakened to the magnificence that is me.

To reclaim the parts of ourselves that have been silenced or forced into assimilation, we must first journey back to the imprint of our spirit. We must trace back to its roots, rediscover its voice, and embrace it as we bring it back to the surface like a long-awaited sunrise.

Our Imprint

When Great-Grandmother Socorro lifted my hands with hers and placed them on my chest, the memories came rushing in, shining light through even the smallest cracks. She reminded me that memory is not only stored in the mind. But what exactly does that mean?

Our spirit has existed before time, long before we manifested into a body. It holds the wisdom of all that ever was. It encompasses the non-physical parts of us, influencing our emotions and our character, which is why I call it "the imprint" of who we are. If the imprint of who we are is suppressed, we will not know freedom. To connect to our imprint is to find our eternal voice, one that is not limited by the physical body or mind.

Colonialism and erasure has detached us from our roots, our history, and our ancient wisdom. It forbade us from knowing ourselves or connecting with the imprints of our souls. It punished us for speaking in our native tongue, for honoring the traditions of our people, and for sharing what we know with our descendants. We have all been impacted by the horrifying acts of colonialism, which is why this work is for everyone, no matter your origin, history, or ancestry. The memory of our spirit, our imprint, can assist us in reclaiming our history, culture, language, ancestral stories, and eternal voice. It is older than our bodies, stronger than muscle, more vital than our organs, and richer than our *sangre*. Within it lies the ancient knowledge of humanity, of the earth and the stars.

In the "Unraveling" process in Offering One, we freed ourselves from all the expectations placed upon us and removed all the layers that told us we did not belong. Now, in the reclamation of our imprint, we are called to remember who we have always been. Though our imprint is older than our bodies, we can use our bodies to access its ancient wisdom.

Reclamation of Our Roots

After I awakened from Great-Grandmother Socorro's visit, the imprint of my spirit cracked open and I remembered things I had never experienced firsthand. These memories were ancient recollections of not just myself, but also my lineage. My great-grandmother's presence allowed me to see the empowering lineage from which I descend. In the reflection of her eyes, I witnessed centuries of women, men, and children from my heritage, all with their hands on my shoulders. I walked with them through the forest of my imprint, with my hands resting delicately upon my chest. My ancestors were all silent, but I could feel their vibrant and empowering presence guiding my spine, supporting my feet in every step I took. Without words, they reminded me I am never alone. No matter what I choose or where I go, there are ancient forces behind me, helping me along the way.

My dream allowed me to see the eternal truth: When we reclaim our cultural and indigenous roots, we cannot be persuaded, pushed around, or forced into silence. It is through this remembrance of who we are and from whom we descend that we are given back our power—the power of voice, wisdom, and memory of our lineage. When we reclaim our roots and culture, we let go of loss, scarcity, and fragility. Our roots sustain us, bringing rich nutrients from the earth of our heritage up through the soles of our feet and infusing our spine, fortifying every bone, pumping every muscle and organ with strength, vitality, and resilience. When our roots flow freely through us, the ancient wisdom of our imprint awakens every cell of our being. With this power, we can never be tamed, no matter how long we've been caged by colonialism, poverty, or abuse.

Colonialism is about disconnection. Remembering and reclaiming are about connection. Growing up, I'd never seen my culture represented in the media, nor was I ever taught the history of my people, our *true* American history. This is the truth for many other communities that do not fit in the rigid shell of a colonized society. No matter how many lies we were told about our history, no matter how far we've been ripped from our cultures, we have the ability to remember and reclaim the imprint of who we are. It never left us. Your imprint is with you, dear friend. It is waiting for you to call it back to yourself. The time is now to reclaim your knowing back to you.

Birthright

As Great-Grandmother Socorro embraced my hands with hers, there was a moment when she looked into my eyes with a stern expression that spoke without speaking: "You know what you are. You know where you come from. You know what you must release."

This encounter scared me at first. It was terrifying to connect with something I'd always sensed, but couldn't fully perceive. I knew that to reclaim, I'd have to let go of what didn't serve me, even if it was all I'd known. And I knew I must move through my fear to get to the truth.

I was told Great-Grandmother Socorro was a woman of few words. What she lacked in verbal expression, she often made up for with food and warm hugs that can *sanar cualquier gripa* (heal any flu), as Apá would say. After meeting her in my dream, I do not think Great-Grandmother Socorro was a woman of few words. I think she was someone who expressed herself through different mediums, in different tones beyond verbal exchanges. We do not need the verbal frequencies of words in order to find our imprint. Words can be felt, experienced, danced, or expressed in many ways. Maybe the times when we find ourselves at a loss for words, it's because we cannot find ourselves at all. When we reclaim our words, they may feel foreign or they might invoke fear. But within our reclamation lies our liberation.

We must use discernment, as there is a difference between being guided by someone or something that considers your wellness, versus being guided by an intruder who wishes you harm. Only the imprint of who you are and those whom you trust should have access to you. Protect yourself and be cautious of who you allow to guide you. Use your intuition.

Our imprint holds our ancient memories that can heal us, hold us, and love us. We access these memories through incantations, practices, and rituals. When we choose to reclaim the imprint of who we are, we can finally quench our thirst, as if drinking from a river rather than a thimble. These memories, this knowing, our imprint—they are our birthright.

Reclamar Practice: Breathwork

To allocate the memory of your imprint, I invite you to do the following breath-work exercise. Take a moment to sit in a comfortable space. Allow your body to relax. Unclench your jaw. Let your shoulders loosen. Relax your hands on either side of you. Gently turn all your attention to your inner sensations. Pay attention to your breathing. Notice how your chest rises and falls through every inhale and exhale. Acknowledge the fuzzy colors and images that wash over your eyes when you close them. Pay attention to the drum of your heartbeat, how its pace changes with each inhale and exhale. In the center of your body—that part where the belly button sits, visualize a tiny floating seed. The seed can take any form or shape with any details that come naturally to your mind. Visualize the tiny floating seed cracking open. Notice that, from the seed, a glowing, blue, spiral orb emerges. Imagine the spiral orb expanding itself, growing bigger and bigger, embracing and surrounding your arms, your legs, your chest, and face. This blue orb that surrounds your body is your imprint. Sit in the knowing of your imprint as long as you desire. When you're ready, allow yourself to wiggle your toes and fingers and open your eyes. Give yourself a hug to welcome the recognition of your imprint.

Y *así es* (and so it is).

Stepping into Alignment

You do not need to be visited by dead relatives for you to connect to your imprint. It's no secret that we live in an environment that is not inclusive and often erases, overlooks, and disproportionately displaces folks. If you have yet to see this, take a moment to ask yourself, dear friend, if you are actively living your truth. Ask yourself these questions:

- Does the society I align myself with honor the imprint of who I am?
- Does it make space for me to express myself?
- Does it encourage and uplift me?

If even one answer to this is "no," then you are not living by the imprint of who you are, and it is time to reclaim and step into what is yours.

Reclamar Journal Prompt

Speak these words out loud, hum them, sing them, or feel them:

I welcome back the parts of myself that became hidden. The imprint of who I am remembers the truth of my voice, my story, my legacy. I am open to this wisdom. I am open to this remembrance.

As you reclaim, ask yourself these questions:

What is my truth?

_____

_____

_____

_____

_____

Deep within, who am I?

_____

_____

_____

_____

_____

What do I wish to reclaim?

_____

_____

_____

_____

_____

What does the imprint of my spirit have to tell me?

_____

_____

_____

_____

_____

Beneath the layers of who I've been told I am, who is it that I've always been?

_____

_____

_____

_____

_____

Let yourself sit with these questions and seek the answers as you venture on the path of reclaiming who you are. Keep your journal by your bed in case you receive messages from your ancestors while you sleep. When you wake up, write down the encounter.

Reclamar Reflection

Reclamation takes work and commitment. Great-Grandmother Socorro did not visit me that day on a whim. She came to me because I had been actively working to dismantle systems that did not honor me. I was intentionally educating myself while unlearning practices and beliefs I had outgrown. I rejected stereotypes and worked diligently to build a loving system within myself. As a detribalized Indigenous Mexican woman who had been detached from her Indigenous traditions, I knew that reconnecting to my roots would bring me closer to the imprint of who I am. I did not know what the process would look like, what the steps were, or how I would go about it. I just knew I had to try. After I did the work of unraveling the harmful parts of myself, I began to reclaim that which uplifted me, encouraged me, made me resilient, and showered me with love. It was the visit of Great-Grandmother Socorro that showed me, it isn't about what you know or what you don't know, memory lives in the spirit—the imprint of

I am the altar at which I pray. I am the Ancestor in becoming. I am the magic and all the chaos. I am purpose and destiny, voyage and arrival, reclamation and truth. I trust in myself and step into my power.

who you are. I encourage you, dear friend, to seek within yourself. Even if you feel fear or uncertainty, I dare you to explore. If you keep going, I guarantee you will remember.

I am the altar at which I pray. I am the Ancestor in becoming.
I am the magic and all the chaos.
I am purpose and destiny, voyage and arrival, reclamation and truth.
I trust in myself and step into my power.

Reclamar Ritual: Ancestral Dream Visit

The following is an invitation to connect with an ancestor through a dream. Like all rituals, you must approach this with deep respect and caution. Not all ancestors wish to be contacted or bothered. Some ancestors are fine with silently watching and not intruding. I highly suggest making sure that you intuitively feel a strong connection to the Ancestor you wish to contact through your dream. You can sense the connection by how your body reacts when you speak about that Ancestor, or how others speak about that Ancestor to you. Does your body feel safe when this Ancestor is brought up in a conversation or when you find yourself thinking about them? Not all ancestors were good ancestors, and some can do more harm than good. Please be sure to do some research on the Ancestor you are trying to contact. Remember, our ancestors do not owe us anything. When we practice sacred reciprocity and show our respect in this ritual through our prayers and intention, our ancestors will feel our respect and choose whether to interact with us.

Here are the steps to invite an Ancestor into your dream to communicate:

- Think of an Ancestor you wish to contact.
- Throughout your day, think about this Ancestor, talk as if that person was in front of you or around you. Envision that Ancestor talking to you. Visualize your Ancestor showing up in your dreams.

- I suggest intentionally praying and writing to this Ancestor in your ancestral journal ten to fifteen minutes before you go to bed. You can also keep an ancestral altar dedicated to this Ancestor where you can spend time before bed praying to them. An ancestral altar can be created by adding totems, images, flowers, or candles to an area of your home dedicated to this Ancestor.
- Go to sleep thinking about the Ancestor you are trying to contact. You can speak the following incantation before you fall asleep to invite your Ancestor into your dream:

> Beloved ancestor (name of ancestor), I come to you with deep respect. I wish to communicate with you and seek your guidance. I call to you (repeat the Ancestor's name three times as you close your eyes and fall asleep).

- Go to sleep with your ancestral journal nearby. When you awaken, grab your ancestral journal and write down any messages you can remember from your dream. Do this right away, before the dream fades. Even if it doesn't make sense, or you only remember fragmented visions, write it down. You never know what may make sense for you later in the day.
- Be patient. You cannot put a time frame on how long it takes for an ancestor to appear in your dream. Some may not have an interest in showing up at all. I suggest doing the steps above consistently for an entire week—though I suggest to always honor your ancestors all year round. It is important to note that we are on our ancestor's clock. They choose when they appear or come with a message. We cannot manipulate or force them to bless us with their presence. Just like anything, the more energy you pour into a particular thing, the more you see its fruits. The same is true in how we honor our ancestors and how they choose to bless us in return.

cultivar

Part Two

Cultivar
(Cultivate)

I come back to my body—soft and strong.

I come back to my voice—direct and calm.

I come back to my feet—rooted and grounded.

I come back to my hands—free and unbounded.

I come back to this warmth.

I come back to this breath.

I come back to this body

and cultivate from all that was hidden.

Y así es (and so it is).

liberar

Offering Three

Liberar
(Liberate)

Incantation

The shame I've carried is not mine to shelter. I release it from my body, I release it from my breath. I release it from my spirit. My truth lies in creating a life free from thoughts that make me feel I must hide or restrict myself. I do not claim shame as my own. I release it and banish it from my home.

Shortened Incantation

I do not let others make me feel ashamed of who I am or whom I wish to be. I see value in being me, and I freely pursue all things that bring me joy.

Liberar,
Una Fábula

In a colorful village, Nina, always full of curiosity, skipped down to the riverbank to cool her feet. As she made her way, she noticed a hidden path that led to a large brick wall. It seemed to touch the clouds, it was so tall. Being the skilled climber she was, Nina quickly scaled the wall without breaking a sweat. When she hopped over to the other side, she was surprised to see that all of the colors were muted. Flowers were gray and had no scent. There were no berry bushes or fruit trees. Instead of crops, a vast stretch of dead, dusty earth stretched before her.

Suddenly, a large beast approached Nina. "Hey, this is *my* land! Trespasser!" The beast had a strange look in his eyes, one that showed a ravenous hunger, even though it appeared that he had consumed every bit of food in the land. The beast growled with rage, pulled back his enormous arm, and hurled a ball of tar at the child. The ball stuck to the girl's back, knocking her to the ground. "Get out!" he shouted. Then he called her a name she had never heard before. The insult made the black tar ball on her back grow larger. It bubbled and oozed, weighing her down.

Before the child could ask what his insult meant, the beast threw another tar ball at her, hitting her in the chest. "Mama! Papa!" the child called, desperately pulling at the heavy black goo.

"No one is coming for you!" the beast snarled. "My wall is too high." The black goo made its way to the child's throat, stifling her screams and even her breath. The tar attached itself to the ground, pulling the child down and trapping her.

Night fell and the girl remained trapped. The beast was asleep in his castle, his snores shaking the stones of the cold, gray building. Nina let out a sigh of surrender and closed her eyes.

As the first light of the sun peaked over the dusty horizon, the girl heard a faint humming sound. She opened her eyes to see a hummingbird twirling in the morning sunlight, proudly shimmering its colorful, iridescent feathers.

"Where are your bright, colorful feathers?" the bird asked. "Why don't you spread your wings and fly?"

"I can't," the girl replied. "I have no wings. The wall is too high and the beast is too strong."

The hummingbird fell on its back with laughter. "I've never heard such nonsense," the hummingbird chuckled.

The hummingbird noticed that the color had gone from the girl's face. "You need some sweet nectar, that will help you get your bright colors back." The bird brought her a flower from the other side of the wall. "Drink!" the bird insisted.

"There is a terrible taste in my mouth from the tar. I can't bring myself to drink." Nina sputtered.

The hummingbird laughed again. "How do you expect to rinse out the sludge of despair from that horrible beast if you don't taste the sweetness of life? Drink!"

Nina put her tongue inside the flower and tasted the nectar.

"There!" said the hummingbird. "You're getting your colors back."

Nina looked at her arms and hands. "I don't see any color."

The hummingbird chirped, "You've got shame in your eyes." The little bird used the hum of its wings to blow away the dried, flaky grime from Nina's eyes. "Now, do you see your beautiful colors?" the hummingbird chirped.

Nina noticed one small patch on her arm that turned blue and green as the light reflected off of it. She took another sip of nectar from the flower and the patch on her arm grew. With each sip, colorful feathers popped out of her skin until she had a full set of vibrant wings.

"Now, fly!" the hummingbird insisted.

"I can't. I don't know how." Nina said, her head down.

The hummingbird giggled. "You don't have to know how, just listen to the song of your ancestors and they'll guide you."

"What song?" Nina asked. "I can't hear anything."

The hummingbird looked at her ears. "Your ears are full of hateful whispers that don't belong to you. It's no wonder you can't hear your ancestors' song of flight." The hummingbird danced in circles around Nina's head until the black smoke of shame swirled out of her ears.

Nina listened. At first, it was faint, but then the song grew. She could hear every voice from every era of her lineage filling up the sky, singing in harmony, the song of flight.

"Now, fly!" The hummingbird shouted. "Fly!"

Nina pulled her body free from the muck of the beast's hatred and shame. Her ancestors' song of flight lifted her wings as she spread them wide.

"You know what to do," the hummingbird whispered.

"Fly," Nina said. As she soared high above the wall, the beast awakened and stomped after her.

"Get back here!" the beast snarled.

But Nina couldn't hear him over the song of her ancestors.

"You never know, a janky car full of Mexicans looks suspicious and could be smuggling illegals or drugs." This was the first time I realized that we were considered a threat to a police officer, his gun pointing at me, my young siblings, and my parents. It was the beginning of our family vacation to the Santa Cruz Beach Boardwalk and a debilitating sense of shame that poisoned me for years.

On a Saturday morning in mid-July, my parents rose before the sun to take us on a summer adventure. We were bubbling with excitement as we hopped out of bed, the soft blue light of the predawn sky glowing behind our curtains. Amá and Apá were used to early mornings. They worked jobs that required both of them to be up and wide-eyed before the sun greeted the day. It was a rare treat that Apá could take the weekend off work, so the whole house was buzzing. It didn't matter that it was 5:00 in the morning, Amá was in the kitchen, making *tortas de chorizo y frijoles* (tortas of chorizo and beans), so we didn't have to spend money on breakfast while on the road. I'm still convinced that the aromas from Amá's kitchen made the sun rise a little earlier that morning. She wrapped the tortas in knitted handkerchiefs for all four of her *chiquillos* (kids), plus extra just in case, and placed them in a cooler with drinks and other snacks. We bounced into my *apá's* 1980s Toyota jalopy and joined the cars full of overworked people on the dimly lit freeway. They were on their way to their boring Saturday jobs, but we were on our way to paradise.

Our joy turned to silence when red and blue lights flashed in our rearview mirror, sparking a glimmer of fear I'd never seen before in my father's eyes. By the time Apá hastily pulled over to the side of the freeway and turned off the engine, the color was completely drained from his once vibrant face. The sweat from his palms made his hands slide down the steering wheel. *"Quédense quietos, yo arreglo esto"* (You all stay put, I'll handle this.), Apá's voice shook. In the side-view mirror, I saw a Caucasian man wearing a cop uniform approaching our car. As the cop got closer to the truck, I could see his right hand resting on a gun that was cinched to his belt. In the light of the new day, it was clear that there was a family inside the truck. He ordered Apá out of the car and took him a few steps away from us, where we couldn't hear their conversation. In the distance, I could only hear echoes of Apá's broken English trying to reason with the cop. Amá turned to me, worried, and told me to help translate for Apá. At sixteen years old, I'd been translating for my parents for many years, but I had never translated for my parents to a cop. Still, I couldn't let Apá fend for himself out there. The truck was a two-door vehicle, so Amá had to get out and lean the seat forward to let me out of the back seat. As I got out of the truck, the cop charged toward us screaming and cussing at me, my mother, and my baby siblings. When I looked up, I saw that he was holding his gun in his hand and pointing it at Amá and me, his eyes squinting in viciousness.

The thing about shame is that it shows up in different ways without our awareness. It trickles down like a waterfall, but rather than cleanse like purifying water, it turns into a swirling vortex, pulling us down and drowning us in the frigid waters of self-loathing. So much of the shame we carry was violently splashed into us by people with hatred in their hearts.

The cop only lowered his gun when I spoke to him in "proper" English and explained that we were just a family going on vacation. But before he let us go, he hit us with a hateful comment that haunted me for years. "A janky car full of Mexicans looks suspicious and could be smuggling illegals or drugs." With his shiny boot of shame, he pushed the trauma of that encounter so far down our throats, we were unable to speak about it for the rest of the drive. I knew that Apá had moved us to Northern California to avoid all the ICE trucks roaming around San Diego, because he said they didn't like people like us. But until that moment, I had never experienced a situation where I, a little sixteen-year-old Mexican girl, was perceived as dangerous. I couldn't comprehend why.

That shiny boot of shame stifled my voice for way too long. I'd internalized the shame of being seen as "dangerous" so far into my being that it changed my reflection in the mirror and every aspect of my life. Shame showed up in my language, my identity, and my body. The hateful words of that cop made me cast down my eyes and lower my head. I wanted to be invisible. If you're invisible, you can't be dangerous enough to have a gun pointed at you by a police officer, right? Invisible people can't be seen as "illegals" or "drug smugglers," right?

Unfortunately, we're not the only family with this kind of story. The shame inflicted upon us by oppressors has caused great harm to marginalized communities, poisoning us from the inside out. That's why we need to embark on quests of personal discovery. We must excavate the shame that has been buried in us by colonizers and hateful authority figures. In Offering Three, we will explore how shame shows up in our language, our bodies, and our identities. I'll offer guidance on how we can release the shame caught in these areas so we can discover who we are underneath and liberate our true selves.

Language Shame

As I spoke English to the cop, telling him that we were on a family trip, Apá grabbed me by the hand, pulling me away. He could tell I was getting frustrated with the officer's interrogations. Apá kept apologizing to the cop. "Sorry." "Sorry." "Sorry."

I didn't understand why he kept saying "sorry." Was he sorry that his young daughter had to speak for him? Sorry he hadn't mastered the "American" language? Sorry for being in a country full of cops who didn't approve of his family? Or was he sorry at his daughter's insolent rebuke of injustice and his powerlessness to protect her? His apologies only aggravated me more.

After the cop finally let us leave, I found myself not only choking on toxic shame, but also feeling confused, afraid, and hurt at seeing my father apologizing for nothing. I was very much aware that the cop pulled us over because of a racist stereotype he believed about Mexican people. And I knew that the cop was in the wrong, not us. Yet, I'll bet anything that he drove away without an ounce of remorse over what he'd just done to an innocent family. Meanwhile, we were all carrying hundred-pound bags of shame around our necks.

After that experience, altering my language became a survival tactic, one that was necessary for my safety. Beautiful, poetic Spanish words that used to roll off my tongue in moments of delight were replaced by, "Sorry." "Sorry." "Sorry." My tone went from bold and boisterous to quiet and tenuous, especially around authority figures. I lost the thrill of a good debate and found myself resigning in the face of disagreement, even among friends and family. I preferred sitting in silence over the excitement of conversation. I even tried to hide my accent, although it would occasionally reveal itself, especially after every "r" in my words. The vortex of shame was drowning my voice. My spirit was reduced to a faint echo that bounced off my teeth in my clenched mouth. My language was hidden in a dark shroud of fear and shame.

I yearned so desperately to blend in that I nearly blended myself out of existence. I hid who I was, the language I spoke, and my distinguishable features that loudly proclaimed, *"she's from alla"* (she's from over there). I not only suppressed my language, but also my ability to stand up for myself, fight for myself, and love myself.

In internalizing the bias that we are "unsafe" or "dangerous," many of us in marginalized communities have learned to distrust ourselves. We become ashamed of what feels natural to us, so we change who we are to make others feel comfortable. Shame in our language isn't only about silencing our words, altering the tone of our voice, or whitewashing our accents. It also makes us believe that *we are the problem.*

Black, Brown, Indigenous folks, and People of Color carry centuries of apologies under our breath, as if our whole existence is an unwanted accident. I grew weary of seeing Amá and Apá apologize to people who spewed phrases like "Go back to your country." I was tired of being picked apart by everyone, including myself. So, finally, I decided that, rather than suppress, silence, or alter my words, I would honor them by radically and intentionally speaking with clarity and truth. That has changed everything for me.

If you've been shamed into silence, or into altering your language, I want you to know it's not your fault. With the incantations in this offering, my intention is to liberate you from ever having to quiet or change your voice again. Our voice must be the vehicle for creating radical change. I know how scary it is to be on the forefront fighting for change when you don't feel understood or welcomed. Please know that I am profoundly grateful to be carrying this effort alongside you. Without this liberation, we will never discover or live by our truth. Our language is radical because it challenges a forced, manufactured status quo that does not serve everyone. Actively honoring our language by speaking or feeling our words with awareness is a powerful way to liberate ourselves.

When we speak with courage and awareness, we embody wisdom. Our words carry enormous worth. They can help us trust ourselves again. Incantations of awareness and wisdom may sound like:

- "I can do this because I believe in myself. I know that I am worthy and capable." This phrase carries the awareness of confidence and self-trust.
- "My opinion matters. I deserve to speak freely, even if my opinions or visions do not perfectly align with others." This phrase carries the awareness of self-expression.
- "I will not let fear stop me from doing what I love. I can always ask for support, so I am not alone in this process." This phrase carries the awareness of honesty and reason.

When we choose words with awareness, we reap the benefits of our language, including honesty, clarity, reason, and support.

Body Shame

As the cop drove away on the day he pulled us over, all I could think about was the way he said "Mexicans," as if he had a chunk of dirt on his tongue he was trying to spit out. Our heritage became a filthy word in his throat, rising up like bile, held behind gritted teeth at first, then spewing out all at once. Once the word was out, he looked uncomfortable, not because he held this hatred, but because he revealed it.

My body internalized the hateful filth spewed on us from that racist cop. I became ashamed of what my brown body represented to others. The only way to survive that trauma was to disconnect from my body. This detachment showed up in how I carried myself, how I dressed, how I took care of my body, and how I engaged in my intimate relationships. The trauma was so painful, I had no choice but to disconnect from the sacred vessel that carries my spirit. Shame coated the inside of my body like a thick goo, gumming up my organs and growing like a tumor, until I found the courage to face the pain and transform it.

When we experience trauma, the body goes into shock. To help us survive, our bodies store that trauma away so we can function. There is a disconnection that happens when our bodies resist or hide the pain of trauma. In some cases, our survival depends on us detaching ourselves from that pain. But there comes a time when we must locate and release it so we can once again be fully connected to our bodies.

Traumatic experiences can cause body dysmorphia, which leads to a negative self-image. Unfortunately, body dysmorphia is all too common, due to the overwhelming expectations rooted in Eurocentric, cisgender standards placed on us by society. Body shaming is centered in racism, fatphobia, ableism, transphobia, and ageism. We have a decades-long history of being forcibly held to a system that thrives on exclusion and privilege. This has left a legacy of pain and trauma in its wake.

External opinions such as those from family, society, media, and so on, influence how we feel about ourselves. How we feel about ourselves affects how we live in our bodies. Reducing how much access negative external sources have to us whenever possible is vital to healing and dismantling the shame our bodies carry. This may look like:

- Reducing our time around family members who constantly hurt us with their uninvited opinions about our bodies.
- No longer consuming media that upholds body privilege and unattainable beauty standards.
- No longer following social media accounts that make us feel bad about ourselves.
- Finding support in a safe community when we've experienced systemic racism, oppression, and hatred.

It is crucial to stay in tune with our bodies and notice what helps them relax or retract. I invite you to make a pact with your body that you will listen to it and honor it. Then build self-trust by following through with that pact.

Every time you listen to your body and treat it with care, you are developing trust between you and your body. That trust is sacred. It will awaken you to the needs of your body. You'll learn to feel your body's cues, knowing when it needs rest, nourishment, nature, protection, release, or to express joy through laughter, dance, or any way the body calls you to. This relationship with your body will lead to healthier internal opinions about you and your worth in this world.

Our bodies are intuitive. If we listen, they will tell us how to heal ourselves. When we are led by doing things that make our bodies feel good, healthy things that bring us vitality, we are removing the muck of internalized shame. This can be challenging if we've become disconnected from our bodies. It may feel embarrassing at first. That's okay. We must remember to meet ourselves with kindness and compassion, gently pushing ourselves out of that familiar shame zone.

Liberar Embodiment Exercise: Shame Extraction

·

LOCATING THE SHAME

In this embodiment exercise, I will guide you to locate and extract any shame present in your body, so you can liberate yourself from the suffering it has caused you.

Find a quiet place where you won't be interrupted. Get comfortable, either by sitting or lying down. Place your hands on your chest or relaxed by your sides. Take a few deep breaths, inhaling through the nose and exhaling through the mouth.

As you breathe, turn your awareness inward. Pay attention to the beat of your heart. Notice your belly rising and falling with each breath. Scan your body, and locate where you might feel stuck. Shame in the body often manifests as tightness or stiffness, hot pain, or even cold areas. Feel free to move your hands over your body to feel the temperature of each area.

·

EXTRACTING THE SHAME:

Once you have located the shame stored in your body, I invite you to do the following:

- Stand up or set your feet firmly on the ground. Visualize the bottom of your feet having small openings in the center. Imagine these small openings becoming larger and larger. (Note: The soles of our feet act as portals to our bodies. Through our feet we can release what we no longer wish to carry in our body.)

- Once the portals of your feet are open, locate the shame in your body. Visualize the shame moving from that area and making its way down to the portals of your feet. (If the shame feels stuck and doesn't want to move, use your hands as magnetic guides to pull the shame from that area. Place your hands on your body and brush your hands over the area that feels stuck in shame until you feel it release.)

- Continue to guide the shame down to the portals of your feet. Once it reaches the soles of your feet, send it through the portals, and release it to the ground. Your shame extraction is complete.

Y *así es* (and so it is).

With this continued practice, I've extracted the shame and trauma that were harming me. I no longer see myself through the eyes of that hateful officer. As it turns out, I am dangerous. I'm a danger to oppressive systems that make us believe lies about ourselves. I'm dangerous in that I provoke radical change that liberates us from oppression. I'm dangerous in being shamelessly aware of who I am and loving every part of me. To oppressors who once benefited from my toxic shame, my liberation is the most dangerous threat imaginable. For them, my freedom is downright terrifying.

Identity Shame

Who we are is not up for debate. We will not pick ourselves apart to uphold views and expectations that diminish the imprint of who we are.

In this truth we live.

Shame can be instilled in our entire existence. It can poison our identities, from how we speak to how we look, from how we act to what we believe, and even whom we love. Shame can overtake our entire existence, making it unbearable to be who we are. It's a harmful and even deadly infection given to us by a society that upholds a rigid system of standards deemed the "correct" way to exist.

While shame used to be a valuable tool in recalibrating us to live in harmony with our communities, it has been distorted into an unnatural state brought on by the oppression of human beings. We were born unashamed. It is our natural state. We cannot get to the root of our imprint if we get pulled into a toxic cycle of self-hatred.

Who we are is not up for debate. This is the truth we must diligently uphold. By being who we are unapologetically, we are extracting the poison of hate we've been fed for centuries. We must cut off the poison source and embrace every bit of ourselves. We will constantly encounter new sources of toxic shame. But if we hold on to our truth with conviction, stating loudly and boldly, *"Who I am is not up for debate!"* we become the antidote to the poison of shame.

May we hold ourselves in unconditional respect. May we never again exclude or silence ourselves, our language, our bodies, or our entire existence, because who we are is glorious and glorious people live shamelessly.

Liberar Practice: Fly

Liberation comes when we allow ourselves to fly despite what may be weighing us down. In this practice we will allow ourselves to fly by creating wings for ourselves.

Find a place outdoors where you feel comfortable to perform the following practice. It is preferable to do this practice during daylight when your local birds are active. (If you live in an area where there are not many birds chirping or humming, feel free to look up bird sounds online.)

- Stand up with your feet firmly planted on the ground. If standing is not an option for you, feel free to sit down. Let your hands rest at your sides and close your eyes.
- Open your ears to receive bird sounds and intently listen to them. Allow the chirping to vibrate through your entire body.
- Let the chirping help you visualize the creation of your own set of wings. Imagine the birdsong as a blue light weaving around you, creating feathered wings that sprout from your back and extend beyond your fingertips.
- Imagine your wings flapping up and down. Continue to connect to the song of the birds. If you are having a hard time visualizing your feathered wings, feel free to extend your arms out and sway them up and down as if they were wings. You can also imagine being transformed into a type of bird to which you feel a strong connection. I like to run around my backyard barefoot during my visualization of my feathered wings. I imagine being transformed into a hummingbird, as this bird is a sacred kin to me.
- As your wings flap up and down, imagine flying above all your pains and worries, seeing that they can no longer hold you down.
- When you are ready, you may fly back down to Earth and plant your feet, wiggling your toes to ground yourself. Offer gratitude to the birds and all the air spirits as you complete this practice. Repeat this practice as often as needed.

Journal Prompts: Shame Release

How can living free from shame impact your life in a positive way?

_____

_____

_____

_____

_____

What does living a life free from shame look like for you? How does it feel? What does it taste or smell like? (Tap into all your senses and explore a shame-free existence).

_____

_____

_____

_____

_____

What can you do right now to feel less shame in your body, language, or in how you see yourself?

_____

_____

_____

_____

_____

Finish the sentence: "When I transform my shame into a powerful reclamation ritual, living free from its shadow I am . . ."

_____

_____

_____

_____

_____

Liberar Reflection

In dismantling and healing the shame others have instilled in us and the shame we've created for ourselves, we can be who we rightfully are. We can embrace every part of ourselves with awareness in our language, cutting off external and internal opinions that do not elevate our understanding of who we are. Countless negative forces will try to redirect us back to the path of shame. But by always holding our truth with conviction, stating *"Who I am is not up for debate!"* and believing in this truth, we will continuously liberate ourselves from toxic shame.

I do not let others make me feel ashamed of who I am or who I wish to be. I see value in being me and freely pursue all things that bring me joy.

As we peel back the layers of all that is unnatural, fearful, and shameful, may we embrace each layer with love and understanding. May we hold them and let them know that we will not exclude our language, our bodies, or our entire existence. Go forth in your glory, dear friend, liberated from shame.

Incantation

I do not let others make me feel ashamed of who I am or who I wish to be. I see value in being me and I freely pursue all things that bring me joy.

Liberar Ritual

SHAME RELEASE DANCE

Shame can be stored in the body, keeping us stagnant, fatigued, and disoriented. Dance is a powerful physical movement that wakes up the body and allows shame to be released. Dance is an expressive practice that can improve emotional wellness and release feel-good chemicals in the brain.

This is an intuitive exercise and does not require specific dance knowledge or choreography. Please move as you intuitively connect to your body and the music. You can move as slow or as fast as you feel called to move. You can either stand or sit down; it is completely up to you.

If it's not accessible for you to move your legs or arms, I invite you to let the song of your choosing guide you internally. Instead of moving your "feet" or "hands," you may move your internal energy. Our bodies are only the shell but our spirit is the ultimate guiding force.

Invite your ancestors to be present with you as you move. Welcome them into this space with you by closing your eyes and asking them to join you for this dance. They can help you move intuitively and assist you in releasing any shame you may carry.

- Start by creating a sacred space around you where your dancing ritual will take place. If I am doing my dancing ritual indoors, I like to light a few candles and dim or turn off the lights of my home to make the space more intimate.

- I find that what we wear in this dancing ritual can be very transformative. Wearing flowy garments such as skirts or dresses can make the ritual extra powerful. As you are moving and dancing to this ritual, you can use the loose fabric of your garment to swirl, throw, wrap, and twist to further help you release the shame (being mindful of candles). I also invite you to use a scarf for this dancing ritual—the scarf can serve as wings.

- Additional but not required: Feel free to bring flower petals, leaves, confetti, or anything that you wish to toss in the air as you celebrate becoming free from shame. Celebrating yourself throughout this entire experience is necessary! (Just be careful of open flames if you've lit candles).

- Play your favorite upbeat song, preferably with no lyrics or singing (a slower paced song can also work if that is what you are drawn to for this ritual) The point of this exercise is to form a connection to yourself through the magic of dance. Lyrics can be distracting when forming a connection to ourselves. However, if there is a song with lyrics with which you strongly connect, please feel free to use it.

- Play the song and let the beat pulse in the center of your heart. Close your eyes and let the sound build in this area. As the energy grows, envision glowing blue lights over your hands, your feet, your chest and back. Imagine the blue lights wrapping around each of these areas spinning with energy.

- Let the glowing blue lights guide your moves as you nurture your connection to the music.

- Once you have a rhythm going, detect any place in your body you may feel shame. (Shame often feels tight, restricted, or shut down).

Once you detect that area of shame, let the glowing blue lights hover over this area. Invite the glowing blue lights to pour into this area and loosen the grip of shame.

- Keep moving, letting the blue lights evaporate any areas of shame in your body.
- When you feel the shame detaching itself from you, bring in your scarf to this part of your ritual. Hold the scarf on opposite ends in each hand, and as you move, allow the scarf to flow behind or in front of you. Guide the scarf to move as if it's a pair of wings. Let this scarf represent the wings you are growing as you liberate yourself from shame.
- Repeat as often and as long as needed.

    Y *así es* (and so it is).

invocar

Offering Four

✦

Invocar
(Invoke)

Incantation

I come from ancient magic that disrupts and heals.
Invoking and reclaiming all that was and now feels.
The love of a new tomorrow and its excitement in awaiting
The cultivation of a life free from baiting.
I invoke within the honor it is to love my spirit.
I invoke within the honor it is to love my body.
I invoke within the honor to love all that I am.

Shortened Incantation

It is not a matter of who I'm not, but who I am that invokes who
I will be.

Invocar,
Una Fábula

Before we are born, we are conjured to this land. A *brujx/e* brings gifts from her garden to her sister, who crafts them in her *cocina magica* (magical kitchen). Every living thing was called to existence by *las hermanas de la tierra* (the sisters of the land). They weave together all the elements in the universe in an intricate spell of creation.

Brujx de la naturaleza gathered the clay from ancient lake beds, the granite from the mountains, the roots from the mighty oak. Then, *brujx de la cocina* took the ingredients her sister brought and combined them in her cauldron. The sisters sang of the alchemy of the bison. As the elements swirled and swelled, the sisters danced and sang the song of creation:

> From the land and sea and stars
> *Invocar, invocar*
> All that is and all we are
> *Invocar, invocar*
> Stone to bone and clay to heart
> *Invocar, invocar*

All life on this land passes through the lips and fingers of *las hermanas de la tierra*. When they called us here, it was with divine purpose and through gifts of the land, sea, and stars. With each new living being comes the potential for another. *Brujx de la naturaleza* (Earth Witches) weaves strands of our hair from the web of the spider and the silk of the worms. They use the patterns of the stars to map out our brains. The sea swirls with the soil to form our blood. The stone from the mountains becomes our bones, the winds breathe life into our chests. The veins from the leaves of the trees become our veins. Amber quartz, brown garnet, and emeralds are polished and imprinted with the galaxies to make our eyes. Vines turn to muscles, and the rings of the trees stamp the tips of our fingers, making prints that bond us with Earth.

Brujx de la cocina combines the gifts of the sisters in perfect measurements to make a child with deep brown eyes and bronze skin. They call on the fire from the sun to ignite her curiosity. They borrow the roar of the lion to rumble within her chest, making her a fierce protector of her family. They take the stillness of the mountain to give her stubbornness and tenacity. They sprinkle the soft petals of the flower to give her a love for beauty. And they bring in the pillows of moss to give her a gentle, compassionate nature.

Invocar
Invocar
Invocar

To know and understand all the parts of her, all her gifts from this land, she must learn from *las hermanas de la tierra*. She must listen to the breeze, so she can hear that the breath within her lungs is the wind in her hair. She must stand on the mountain to feel the strength of her bones. She must gaze at the stars to perceive the galaxies in her mind. Everything she is, everything we are, is of this magical universe. We were gathered and sung into existence. Before we are born, we are conjured to this place, cultivated with intention from the land, sea, and stars.

I grew up hearing my *abuelas*, *tias*, and *amá* sing and hum while they cooked and cleaned, their colorful aprons wrapped around the mountainous curves of their bodies. With their hands smeared in all kinds of spices and *masa* (dough), they laughed and chattered about everything under the sun and moon. Their facial expressions occasionally perked up with surprised looks followed by *"No me digas que fue el?!"* (Do not tell me it was him?!). Across the kitchen, one of my aunts would be stirring *los frijoles* (the beans) as she unleashed a vivacious laugh, harmonized with a slight wheeze. And somewhere in the back of the kitchen, my *abuela* hummed her favorite Chavela songs as she peeled back the husks of the *elotes*. Her hum held us in a beautiful background melody that pulled together the entire scene, the entire world, in our aroma-filled kitchen.

I can recite every *clink* and *clank* of the pot symphony in Amá's kitchen. I know them by heart and soul. I know that she stores the pots in her dishwasher because who actually uses their dishwasher? At least not in this Mexican household! And if the pots are not in the dishwasher, then, you guessed it! They are in . . . the oven. I know Amá is the ultimate recycler, because she keeps every empty butter bin and empty sauce jar for storing seasonings and leftovers. I would nag at her to get rid of them, but she would always say *"Nosotros no somos desperdisiosos"* (We are not wasteful). I love this about Amá, how she refuses to get rid of anything simply because the use for which it was intended has been completed. She always finds new ways to bring purpose to things that would have otherwise been discarded. Amá sees the value in everything and chooses to love it all. Being in Amá's kitchen showed me how love lives in every ingredient, every container, every hum, and every story.

Growing up, I've watched countless people gather in Amá's kitchen. My *abuelas* and tias (grandmothers and aunts) have had hard conversations there.

I've seen laughter fill the entire room. It's the home of our early morning sunbathing rituals, Amá and I soaking up the light from the window above the kitchen sink with a *cafecito* (coffee) in hand. I have seen my relatives give pieces of themselves to the meals they cook. Amá softens in the kitchen. In this magical place, the border she's built around herself crumbles, one brick at a time. The kitchen is Amá's haven, the place where she can profoundly love herself and silence her inner critic. It is in the kitchen where I know Amá discovered she was a *bruja* (witch). All witches discover their magic either in nature or in a kitchen. My magic radiates from both places.

Our kitchen has always been the place where the ultimate invocation and cultivation happen. It is where Amá taught me about alchemy. At first, I only applied these lessons to food. Later, I realized how we can also cultivate a practice of healing, invoking self-love and self-respect. Spending time in the kitchen led me to honor rituals and sacred formulas that I carry into my incantations and embodiment exercises.

This offering is about invoking the spirit of *amor propio* (self-love). If you are like me, *amor propio* was not modeled for you. But that's okay, because we can learn to do it for ourselves. For me, growing up, love showed up in nonverbal ways, through nourishment of our bodies, hard work, and quiet glances. I have been fortunate to witness the invocation of love taking place in many kitchens of my family members. What happens in the kitchen is an unassuming magical process, one in which you can see the spirit of *amor* fluttering through the entire space. These moments taught me about *amor* and the different ways we can express it.

Invocar Embodiment Exercise

PURIFY

Just as we begin by washing our hands before we prepare a meal, purifying them and getting them ready for what is ahead, we can also purify our minds, bodies, and spirit to receive healing and abundance. To create a self-loving practice, we must cleanse ourselves of any residue we've picked up throughout the day, week, month, or year. We must clear ourselves of the dirt of external opinions, wash off the expectations of others, gently cleanse away internal shame, and rid ourselves of toxic negative perceptions. When we come to the next phase of our ritual, we will be clean, clear, and ready to work with ingredients that will nourish our spirit.

Some ways you can cleanse yourself:

- Bathe or shower: Imagine the energy you've picked up throughout the day washing off your body and swirling down the drain, leaving you refreshed and clear.
- Grounding: Sit outside with your bare feet on the grass or soil. Breathe in the cleansing elements of nature. Imagine the negativity moving down through your feet and into the earth, where it will be cleansed and turned into plant food.
- Breathing: Breathe in clean air and fresh energy. Breathe out any negativity you've picked up.

GATHER

When preparing a meal, we gather ingredients—we reclaim elements from the earth that will combine with one another to create something delicious. This can symbolize the practice of cocreating with someone and reclaiming the gifts of the earth. Each ingredient might be limited on its own. The alchemy of the kitchen teaches us that magical things can happen when we combine the right ingredients and use the proper tools. Each ingredient contributes to the success of the next ingredient. The process of combining ingredients to make something extraordinary is incredibly powerful. In your practice, gather items for your altar, your sacred space, and combine them to invoke the delicious energy they have to offer. (You can learn more about creating an altar in Offering Five: *Encantar* [Enchant].)

●

BUILD

We build by picking our proteins—the part that offers us strength and persistence. In any practice, we need strength and persistence to maintain our momentum. I grew up hearing Amá preach to her children that eating proteins *te hacen mas fuerte* (makes you stronger). As an adult, I now understand that proteins are an important part of our diets. They are the building blocks of our bodies. In our spiritual practice, we also need essential building blocks.

I made an invocation list of ways to strengthen my body and improve the health of my mind and spirit. This list travels with me wherever I go, so I can pull it out to remind myself as needed:

- **Invoke body strength:** Get active! When we physically feel strong, we feel confident. True confidence is born from overcoming obstacles and realizing your strength.
- **Invoke mind strength:** I define mindfulness as a conscious awareness that transforms our feelings and experiences into nurturing and gentle rituals. When we are mindful of our thoughts, words, actions, environment, what we consume, and who we are around, we can filter out people, places, and things that do not serve us.

- **Invoke spirit strength:** When the spirit is strong, so is every other part of us. There are many ways that you can build your spiritual strength, such as meditation, yoga, being creative, being with loved ones, spending time in nature, or volunteering your time to organizations you care about. One of my favorite ways to build my spiritual strength is by spending time outdoors. Time in nature is good for your health. Within our bodies, we carry all the elements of nature, so being outdoors fuels the spirit. I recharge my spirit by connecting it to the elements of my body: Earth, Fire, Air, Water (more about these in Offering Five).

Fueling ourselves with practices that build our strength system is vital to the evolution of our *amor propio* (self-love) practice. With the strength that we build physically, emotionally, and spiritually, we develop the capacity to release what doesn't serve us and invoke all that is best for us.

·

CRAFT

In the kitchen, pots and pans are vessels to help us craft a practice of nourishment. This can also represent our physical bodies. Our bodies are the essential vessels for our spirit. We must show gratitude to our bodies and honor the magic of creation that pumps through our veins. Just as pots are used for boiling and cooking, our bodies process messages from our senses, thoughts, feelings, and experiences.

Honor Your Vessel—The Body

- The body loves water! Water is restorative, healing, and purifying. Seek out bodies of water in nature. Find sacred water ways and offer gratitude to your body by saying: "Thank you, body, for being the container of all the wonderful things happening inside me. You are strong, brilliant, and beautiful, and I adore you for allowing me to experience this life with you as my shield."

- Treat yourself! Let your body take pleasure in the things it enjoys. Wear fabric that feels good on the skin. Eat a delectable dessert, mindfully tasting each bite on your tongue. Run a feather up and down your skin. Awaken your body to pleasure.
- Body massages are incredibly healing. Not only do they release tension within the body, but they also calm the mind. Massages are a great way to show our bodies gratitude for everything they do for us.

By showing gratitude to our bodies, we are actively invoking an *amor propio* (self-love) practice that is built on a foundation of appreciation, not expectation.

SPICE

Finally, we add the ingredients that offer flavor, love, enrichment. Your enrichment can be as unique as you are. It is okay to add our own personality and playfulness to these practices. We can curate them to look and feel the way we wish.

Seasonings: Taste the Rich Flavors of Life:

In our *amor propio* (self-love) practice, we must find the things that make our bodies, minds, and spirits come alive. Experiencing art is a delightful seasoning for me. When I need a bit of zest in my life, I'll visit a museum, see a play, or listen to live music. Creativity is the spice of life. Without art, culture, music, and dance, our lives would be dull and tasteless. Playfulness can also spice up your spirit. When we find ways to play like we did when we were children, we remember the flavors of our carefree childhoods. Seasoning is crucial for a healthy spirit.

Amor propio doesn't have to look any particular way, it just has to make sense to you. We are free to cultivate a rich, nurturing practice that invokes an ancient wisdom and love into our bodies, minds, and spirits. Like our ancestral *brujx/es*, we combine elements that breathe new life into our beings, awaken our senses, and give us strength to overcome obstacles. With our unique *amor propio* practices, we can create medicine, healing, and nourishment that will sustain us throughout our lives.

You do not need to come from a loving household or upbringing to learn how to build a loving relationship with yourself. Love is accessible to all of us. It is within and all around us. Even in the smallest things we do every day, we can always glimpse love. In a society that has ripped us apart and convinced us there is nothing to love about ourselves, may we remember that we always have the ability to invoke love in big ways and small. Without this essential ingredient, we have nothing.

Invocar Practice

CREATE YOUR *AMOR PROPIO* (SELF-LOVE) MENU

Everyone's *amor propio* menu is different, depending on our needs and desires. Just as with food, some may prefer menudo, while others like *tortas*. Some may not be able to tolerate certain foods or spices. This menu should be particularly crafted for your own use in a way that considers your needs.

Now, let's stock our shelves with ingredients to aid us in building our *amor propio* practice. An *amor propio* practice is a living, dynamic thing. It will ebb and flow like the sea. It will change with the seasons. Some days, it will feel light like the breeze. Other times, it will seem heavy like a mountain. This process does not have to look pretty, it may even feel uncomfortable at times. Consider the process of cutting onions for a dish. We may cry, our eyes may burn, but once the onion is combined with the rest of the ingredients, it adds flavor and aroma that make a delicious dish.

We must understand that it may take time for many of these practices to feel comfortable doing. But as we continue to live by these practices, our bodies will slowly adapt, and we will experience the benefits.

Here is my collection of ingredients that I use in my *amor propio* practice:

- A playlist of songs that embrace me in their lyrics and rhythm. They are songs of intimacy, playfulness, or encouragement. I listen, dance, and sing to them.
- An *amor propio* journal. As soon as I wake up, I write one thing about myself for which I am grateful. I let my entry affect the way I move through my day.
- Mirror gazing has been transformative for me. I spend time looking at myself in the mirror, paying attention to every detail of my body. I speak loving words to myself, such as, "I am proud of you," "I am so happy you are who you are," "Thank you for not giving up," "You are everything I've ever hoped for," "You don't always have to be strong." I repeat these loving phrases as often as needed.

- Ten minutes of direct sun contact. The sun is a natural mood-booster.
- Laughter is medicine, literally! Laughter stimulates our organs, such as the heart, muscles, and lungs.[2] It lightens the mind and enhances the spirit. Having a laughing practice helps us feel confident. It releases tension. I like to watch comedy specials or invite friends over to share our best "jokes." This ingredient can be transformative.
- A hearty and nourishing, home-cooked meal. Feeding our bodies foods that tickle our taste buds and make us feel good is a great way to show appreciation to ourselves. I love eating soups for this exercise. Warm foods make my body feel loved. (See below for an *amor propio*).
- Daily incantations with an erasable marker on a mirror to express love for myself. Mirrors are great reflective tools. When we offer our reflection messages of love and respect, our reflection sends those messages back to us.

These are just a few rites or "ingredients" that you can add to your *amor propio* practice. We can always add, alter, or shift our practice, depending on how we feel. The most important thing to remember when building an *amor propio* practice is that it must be allowed to evolve. Do what honors the imprint of your spirit. Just like any recipe, not all ingredients will work together in harmony. Choose ingredients or practices that fit the recipe you envision for yourself. Let your desire guide you.

Amor Propio Tea Potion Recipe

Tea is a great way to show appreciation and infuse love into your body. Here is my personal recipe that I often come back to when I am in need of some *amor propio*.

What you'll need:

- Three or four rosebuds, fresh or dried. The rose is the ultimate love flower. Roses symbolize passion, admiration, and love.
- A quarter teaspoon of ground cinnamon. Cinnamon carries cleansing, purifying, and protective properties. It is a great addition to this potion, as cinnamon will cast off any intrusive energies, and purify and protect you with its loving charm.
- One-eighth teaspoon of ground clove. Clove has many magical properties. For this potion, we are using the healing properties of clove to find the magic in relationship with ourselves.
- One tablespoon of honey. Honey represents sweetness and pleasure. For this potion, we are infusing the sweetness of love with our bodies.
- A half cup of water. Water is purifying and nourishing. We let the cleansing power of water nourish our mind, body, and spirit.
- One cup of preferred milk. Milk symbolizes motherhood and abundance. We let the mother energy gently cradle us as we drink this potion.

VISUALIZATION

Put all of your ingredients together and drink your *amor propio* potion tea. While you drink, I invite you to envision the tea sliding down your throat as pink-colored energy. Imagine it flowing down to your belly, out to your arms and down to your legs. Envision your entire body glowing from this energy, making you feel protected, nourished, and loved.

INCANTATION

I invite you to recite the incantation from the beginning of this chapter to awaken the magic of this potion tea. You can recite the incantation before you begin drinking your potion or once you have finished it. Here it is again:

I come from ancient magic that disrupts and heals.
Invoking and reclaiming all that was and now feels.
The love of a new tomorrow and its excitement in awaiting
The cultivation of a life free from baiting.
I invoke within the honor it is to love my spirit.
I invoke within the honor it is to love my body.
I invoke within the honor to love all that I am.

Shortened Incantation

It is not a matter of who I'm not, but who I am invokes who I will be.

Amor Propio Invocar Journal Prompts:

Ask yourself these questions as you build your *amor propio* practice:

What brings me happiness and why?

_____

_____

_____

_____

_____

What makes my body feel good?

_____

_____

_____

_____

_____

What about myself am I grateful for?

_____

_____

_____

_____

_____

What fills me with excitement and anticipation?

_____

_____

_____

_____

_____

What brings my spirit peace?

_____

_____

_____

_____

_____

What feels like safety for me?

_____

_____

_____

_____

_____

When I embarked on my self-loving journey, it was important for me to have many conversations with myself. I would speak or write to get clear on what I was inviting in and why. Whenever I felt the grime of negativity, such as impostor syndrome, I would sit with these emotions and work through them, using one of my cleansing practices mentioned previously.

Invocar Reflection

Amor propio is a practice that many of us were not taught. It may have been confused with egocentricity or self-centeredness. But the truth about *amor propio* is that it's about compassion toward ourselves. In a world filled with constant swells of hatred, it is vital we practice *amor propio* as a gesture of compassion and kindness toward ourselves as we navigate these choppy waters.

Our *amor propio* practice will continue to expand the more we walk this path. Some ingredients will change while others will become essential. It is important to pay attention to how you feel in your *amor propio* practices. Just like any kitchen, your *amor propio* menu will be filled with many ingredients, cultivated to perfection. Some days you will be in need of a comforting hot soup, and other days may call for a light fruit salad. As you continue to build your menu, you will have a variety of ingredients ready to create a delicious recipe that is nourishing and loving to your mind, body, and spirit.

It's not a matter of who I'm not, but who I am
that invokes who I will be.

Incantation

It is not a matter of who I'm not, but who I am that invokes who I will be.

Amor Propio Invocation Ritual

•

"AMOR PROPIO AMULETO" (SELF-LOVE AMULET)

In this exercise, we will be creating an *amuleto* (amulet) with the intention of cultivating love for ourselves. *Amuletos* have been used by many cultures. People wear or carry them to keep something away or to bring something forth. In this ritual, I will show you my own personal amulet that I have been creating for years now. It has brought me immense amounts of love.

Things to gather for this exercise:

- A piece of cloth, any kind of fabric (we will be stitching this piece of fabric into a small pouch). Make sure the fabric is strong enough to hold items inside the pouch. You can make it more fun by using a pink piece of fabric (pink represents self-love).
- A needle and thread. Any color of thread will work. Feel free to gather colors you love. (If you do not have access to needle and thread, fabric glue is also an option.)
- A cord for hanging the pouch around your neck.
- A piece of paper and pen, pencil, marker, or paintbrush.
- One or two small items that represent love for you and that can fit in the *amuleto* pouch (for example, a flower, a piece of jewelry, a stone or crystal, herbs, etc.).
- A ribbon (any color that speaks to you).

Putting it all together:

- Cut your fabric into two equal-sized squares.
- Stitch or glue the fabric into a pouch large enough to hold your gathered items, but small enough to hang comfortably from your neck. Leave one side open for your items.
- Set your intentions as you stitch. Turn your thoughts to what self-love means to you and how it feels to love yourself.
- Attach a cord to the pouch so you can hang it around your neck.
- *Voila!* You have your very own *amor propio* pouch! (Remember: This doesn't have to look perfect, it is the little mishaps that add character to our crafts. You want this to be as personalized as possible.)
- On your piece of paper, write in the present tense the love you wish to invoke and embody every day. (Even if it may not be true for you yet, writing it in the present tense helps us channel that energy and eventually leads us to becoming it). For example: "Everything I do and everywhere I go, I let love lead the way. I willingly trust the love I feel and know that it will not misguide me." Your statement can be as long or short as you wish. Do what feels right for you. When you are done, fold it into a square and place it inside your *amuleto* pouch.
- Place your gathered items into your amulet pouch with your note. As you place them inside the pouch, say out loud or in your mind what each item resembles in your *amor propio* practice. It is important to let these items know their meaning so they can work on their purpose as you carry them in your *amuleto* pouch. For instance, "This flower represents gentleness toward myself," or "This crystal represents the beauty I see in myself."
- Feel free to add anything else that represents self-love for you. Once you are done adding all your items, tie the ribbon you gathered around the opening of your *amuleto* pouch to close it. Again, as you

tie your *amuleto* pouch with the ribbon, keep in mind what this *amuleto* pouch is doing for you. In fact, throughout this entire process, keep *amor propio* in your mind.

Here is a picture of my *amor propio amuleto* pouch for inspiration:

Y *así es* (and so it is).
Your ritual is complete.

revelación

Part Three

Revelación
(Revelation)

"I will sing you out like a rib that no longer fits and pour you like fine *mezcal* in a goblet made for kings and queens. I will comb your hair and whisper secrets of the paradise made for you and me. We are *santa magia, pura divina*, deserving and worthy to receive what has always been for us. *Abuela dice que la revelación viene*, when we no longer see through the eyes of those who never seen the gold in ours."

—TO THE *ABUELAS*,
WHO TAUGHT US NOT TO GIVE A FUCK

encantar

Offering Five

Encantar
(Enchant)

Incantation

I invite creativity to enchant me if I feel I have lost my ways. I invite creativity to enchant me so I may understand the language of my spirit. I invite creativity to enchant me so I may know what it means to exist in this body, in this time, in this moment. I invite creativity to enchant me without any expectations, and I trust that it will lead me to my highest expression of who I am.

Shortened Incantation

I invite creativity to enchant me so I may always find myself and fully harness the power of my spirit.

Encantar,
Una Fabúla

Before time began, before our ancient ancestors were given earthly bodies, before we came to know the blessings of Madre Tierra (Mother Earth), we were the enchanted prayers of the Elemental Spirits. To bring forth their sacred legacy of life, the Elemental Spirits came together to pray us into existence.

Padre Fuego (Father Fire) soared through the infinite universe, searching for a home for his deepest wish. He fell in love with Madre Tierra and asked for her blessing to land his comet body on her soil. She invited him in, and with deep gratitude, he released his prayer of life into the depths of her being. They became one, and thus began the cocreation of life.

Their loving collision awakened the water that had been asleep for eons, deep in Madre Tierra's womb. Agua Bendita (Holy Water) bubbled up to the surface, her elixir blessing Madre Tierra with a fertile landscape of green, blue, rust, and gold. Seeds formed and sprouted.

Under the silver light of a full moon at midnight, abundant young leaves pushed through Madre Tierra's skin, creating a lush green landscape. Vines unfurled and stretched across the curves of her mountains, expressing their gratitude in tiny buds with velvet petals.

Viento de Tempestad (Storm Wind) swept across the vines, excited by the beautiful young buds. The wind spirit approached with curiosity. He noticed there was something inside the buds, held tightly within the petals. Viento de

Tempestad whistled an enchanted prayer onto the vines, coaxing the tender petals to open and reveal their hidden treasure.

In the center of the flowers, tiny earthly bodies curled together. Viento de Tempestad breathed spirit into the bodies, as they stretched and unfolded their arms and legs. "Breathe me in and release, young beings. Spirit lives within you now." Suddenly, their senses were full of energy.

They heard the whisper of Agua Bendita, saying: "From my warm springs, you are alive. I am you, you are me."

From the deep caves beneath their bodies, they heard Madre Tierra chant, *"Cuerpito, cuerpito que lindo eres. Eres tierra y yo vivo en ti"* (Little one, little one, how lovely you are. You are Earth, and I live within you).

And from the center of their chests, they felt the spark from Padre Fuego igniting within them a serene warmth they came to know as love.

At last, the earthly bodies of our ancient ancestors, enchanted and crafted from the prayers of the Elemental Spirits, were alive and at home.

Note: This offering is structured a little differently than previous offerings. We will be discussing the elements of the earth, with insights and exercises pertaining to each element. The four elements—Earth, Air, Fire, and Water—will each have their own section in this offering. Within each section, we will discuss the ancient wisdom of the element, the creative teachings of the element, the creative practices to connect with the element, and a journal prompt or exercise pertaining to the element. You will come away from this chapter with a knowledge and appreciation of each element in nature, as well as an elemental art altar of your own.

Las manos de mi abuela (my grandmother's hands) are bronze, with galaxies of tiny freckles sprinkled over every crease and wrinkle. She likes to adorn each finger with gold rings that hold vibrant gems and flower designs. I like to watch her as she paints every fingernail with her favorite bright color of the moment. I love seeing the way Abuela tends to her hands, how she honors every wrinkle and freckle, as if declaring, "Look at me! Look at all I've done! Look at all I've created and held!"

"Las manos," as she says, "son los portales de la creatividad de uno" (The hands are the portals of one's creativity). "Mis manos han pasado por mucho pero gracias a ellas he podido sobrevivir" (My hands have been through a lot, but because of them, I have been able to survive).

Abuela was born in 1932 in Compostela Nayarit, in the coastal lands of Mexico. She is Amá's mother, a tejedora (weaver), and a sensible and nourishing, Virgo, earthly woman. She is the woman who taught me what it means to be a creative. Having grown up with little to no income, Abuela says her crafty ideas came from her creative instincto (instinct). Abuela is a tejedora. The blankets she's weaved, the skirts, and *cervilletas* (napkins) she's adorned with colorful *bordados* (embroidery), all make up a beautiful collection; heirlooms that have been passed down to me. Nobody taught her how to weave or do embroidery. She says she was guided by an inner knowing. *Mi abuela* taught me that, in the absence of a skilled master, we can be our own guides and teachers. If we allow ourselves to be guided by the *instincto* (instinct) within, we can discover how much the body and our imprint know. *Instincto* may graciously lead the hand, fill the throat with song, or move the feet. I believe *mi abuela* was moved by something ancient and ancestral within her that guided her creativity.

When I was twenty-five years old, I found myself severely overworked, stressed, and depleted. As a fresh college graduate, I was working multiple jobs and had been recently diagnosed with a chronic illness. On top of that, I also faced the newfound pressure of finding a career in my field. Many children of immigrant parents shoulder the heavy pressure to "make it," to prove our parents' struggles were worthwhile. I craved a space to be held, supported, and understood. One day, as I was reading *Loose Woman: Poems*, a collection of poems of love, sex, and womanhood by Sandra Cisneros, I remembered what *mi abuela* had said about *instincto*. Something about the enchanting words in that book awakened my spirit. Suddenly, I couldn't get enough of poetry. I devoured it every chance I got. Eventually, I decided to write poetry of my own. Writing led me to drawing. I'd often pair an illustration with a poem to add to the meaning. I wrote and wrote, getting lost in the enchantment of poetry, tapping into an ancient knowing—an ancestral wisdom that was guiding my hand and my words. Sure, I had drawn a few times in my life and written essays for school, but it was never in my own unique style. This time, I expressed myself from my creative *instincto*. I let my spirit lead the way.

Writing and illustrating quickly became familiar concepts, as if I had known them my entire life. The more I made time for them, the more I connected to a strange, yet familiar consciousness within me. Poetry and art not only helped me cope, heal, and express myself, they also connected me to an ancient, creative force that came alive in my body. Abuela knew the value in making time for creativity. She knew that through creativity, we can unlock the ancestral ways of communication—the ancestral collective consciousness. It is through the process of expressing our creativity that we live by the truth of our imprint. Creativity can help us make sense of our exterior and interior worlds. It's a physical manifestation of the invisible universe, where the external and internal collide.

Ancient and modern-day civilizations understand the importance of creativity, which is why they've fought to preserve their cultures, traditions, foods, languages, songs, and stories—many of which could have been destroyed due to colonialism, genocide, and erasure. My ancestors, who are the Huichol Indigenous Peoples—one of the indigenous groups from Nayarit, Mexico—centered their creative practices around painting, sculpting, and embroidery. They combined yarn and beaded embroidery to create folk art pieces with intricate patterns and designs that carry a spiritual or cultural significance. All of our ancestors are creatives. They have preserved their stories through creative mediums for us, as their descendants, to know of them and thus know ourselves.

The Creative Enchantment of Madre Tierra

Creativity is found all around us. Madre Tierra (Mother Earth) is the ultimate creative force. She paints rainbows across the skies, she blows gusts of winds to make leaves swirl and dance, scattering brilliant color palettes across the mountains, fields, and forests. Madre Tierra is the ultimate artist, teaching us through the beauty of her own creativity. Abuela often turned to Madre Tierra to enchant her *instincto* with inspiration. Abuela worked in sacred harmony with Madre Tierra to express herself, and make beautiful creations to help her provide for her family. Abuela would forage the abundant lands, harvesting vegetables, plants, and herbs to make nourishing meals for her family when groceries were scarce, her *instincto* (intuition) guiding her along the way.

Connecting to our Madre Tierra is a powerful way to spark creativity and connect to the ancient wisdom of our ancestors. Ancestral wisdom lives within all of us. Sadly, many of us struggle with connecting with our ancestors due to colonialism, genocide, and erasure. But it is by connecting to Madre Tierra that I have been able to form the most profound connections with my ancestors. We carry all the elements of Madre Tierra in our bodies. Therefore, coming back to Madre Tierra allows us to connect to ourselves.

The Sacred Circle of Elements

Forming a relationship with the elements can be a wonderful way to connect to the ancestral creativity that lives within us. Each element—Air, Water, Fire and Earth—has something profound to teach us about ourselves. They show us how connecting to the essence of each element can help us build an inspiring, creative practice that connects us with everything around us. In this offering, we will explore each element's spirit, wisdom, and teachings to formulate unique creative practices. Creativity is not only important for the preservation of our cultures but also for the survival of human, animal, and plant species. We've become severely disconnected from nature and have therefore lost a deep connection to ourselves. By returning to creativity, we are enchanting ourselves with the spirit of our ancestors and tuning into the imprint of who we are.

Air

The element of air moves through all land-based plants and animals on this planet. It wisps in and out of our mouths, noses, even our skin. Our skin literally breathes. Although we usually cannot see it, air is all around us, constantly providing us with renewing oxygen so our bodies can thrive.

Air is the element of communication. It carries our stories, songs, and laughter to the ears of our loved ones. Seeds travel from one place to another through air to ensure diversity in nature. Winged creatures are carried by the winds. We can use air to ground ourselves through our breath and connect to our internal worlds and imaginations. Air allows us to interact with our environment, ourselves, and one another.

※

ANCIENT WISDOM OF AIR

Air is the carrier of everyone's prayers and incantations. It is a powerful conduit, for we are constantly in contact with its energy. Air is the ultimate spell caster, invocator, and initiator, as all spells and words fly through it to be manifested. Air teaches us the ancestral wisdom of being a constantly renewing vessel—to carry ourselves with delicacy and pride. With every breath, we hold and share the knowledge, love, and brilliance of our ancestors and of our Madre Tierra. Air leads us to become all that is intended for us—a destiny of our own making.

※

CREATIVE TEACHING OF AIR

Air is a crucial part of our creativity as it is connected to our imagination—the part of us that detaches itself from the physical form to connect with the energy around us. It is also connected to our imprint or spirit, as air is the bridge between our external and internal worlds.

When we focus on our breath in meditation, we are connecting to our higher selves—our spiritual selves. Our higher selves contain a knowledge that is free from judgment, worry, and speculation. I call this part of ourselves the wisdom of our ancestors, as I believe that our higher selves are our ancestors. When we access this part of ourselves through breath, we are in direct communication with an all-knowing presence, whether we call it our ancestors, God, or our enlightened self.

Creatively, air teaches us the importance of being in our imaginative state. It provides space for us to create. It lives in the moments between thoughts, the flutter of a seed as it floats by, the whisper of tree branches. In this sacred space, there is no need to force or grasp anything. Air is abundant, all around us, there for us when we need to take our next breath. It does not linger. It flows out of our lungs when we are ready to release it. Our imaginative state is closely linked with the element of air. Spending time in our imaginative state allows us to bring the magic of our internal worlds into the physical world. It is from the playground of our imaginations that we innovate new ideas, dream of new possibilities, and solve complex problems. Anytime we wish to visit our imaginative state, all we have to do is focus on our breath.

CREATIVE PRACTICES WITH AIR

Working with air requires us to trust what we cannot physically see, and shift our focus inward to be led through our creativity journeys. Here are a few ways you can work with the element of air through imagination:

- **Imagination building:** One of my favorite practices is using my imagination when I wake up in the morning. I start by gazing at something in my environment. This can be something right in front of me, or a scenic view out my window. I start by acknowledging every detail in my view, paying attention to all the sensations I am feeling as I explore. Once I've acknowledged every detail, I invite my imagination to participate. For example, when I am thoughtfully gazing upon a scenic view, I may pay attention to the veins of the leaves, the atmosphere, the colors, and the movement of nature. Then I invite my creativity to play. I'll place imaginative figures in the view. Sometimes, the figures are children running through the foliage. I may listen to all the nature sounds as the children frolic and play. Or maybe, on a hot day, I'll imagine an eagle with ten eyes flying across the sun because the heat makes my face feel like it's melting. There are no rules. You can create whatever you want. When you allow your imagination to dream up impossible, unreal things, it strengthens your creativity. After this practice, I like to either journal about my experience, draw, sing, dance, or cook. I finish by offering gratitude to the air that surrounds us, taking a deep breath, and filling my lungs.

Water

Considering that our bodies consist of about 60 percent water, it makes sense that we are incredibly attuned to this element. For centuries, people all over the world have had a deep connection to water, often traveling great distances to bathe in waters known to be transformative. Without a doubt, we are deeply connected to the element of water. We spend our first living months growing in the nourishment and protection of our mother's water-rich womb. It is in water that we were created, and in water where we come back to reconnect with our truth.

ANCESTRAL WISDOM OF WATER

Water is a powerful guide that can cleanse emotions and thoughts that hurt the body. When negative thoughts and feelings stay trapped in the body, we may fall ill, feel stressed or depressed, experience mind fog, or disconnect from our spirituality. Water moves and restores energy in the body, carrying away negative thoughts or stagnant energy like a stream that rolls down a mountain.

Water represents consciousness, because it is where all life begins. It purifies our bodies internally and externally, allowing us to see the truth of our imprint. This is why water is reflective, acting as a mirror—constantly reminding us to look deeper within and access the pure consciousness that flows through us.

CREATIVE TEACHINGS OF WATER

Water teaches us about clarity with its purifying energy, which leads us to the true nature of life and creativity. It can be still or in constant motion, held in a container, or drip from our palms when we collect it in our hands. It takes the shape of the vessel that holds it, reminding us to adapt to our surroundings. The power of water can erode mountains, teaching us patience and persistence. Water is the ultimate shape-shifter, turning solid like ice or snow, liquid like rivers and lakes, or it can become vapor in the sky. The hush of the ocean waves can soothe our souls, but a flood from a rainstorm can be terrifying. This element holds a powerful essence of creativity.

Water teaches us the importance of inspiration. This element shows us that by trusting our internal and physical rhythms that rise and fall like the tides, we can be in harmony with the moon, stars, planets, and nature. It shows us that new ideas can be found all around us and within us. This magical element is a portal to the deep secrets of our planet, where corals and chasms support life we have yet to discover.

CREATIVE PRACTICES WITH WATER

Water is a powerful guide that can attune you to your highest inspiration and creativity. Below is my favorite practice for working creatively with water. Feel free to use this practice in whatever way best fits your needs.

- **Summon the energy of inspiration**: To find inspiration, I invite you to rinse your feet and/or hands with water. I like to do this outdoors by grabbing my water hose and letting the water wash over my hands and feet. Our hands and feet are extensions of our imprint. They hold their own consciousness, which extends outside of us with intention and love. By letting water flow over these parts of us, we are reawakening their consciousness to create, dance, write, and express. I like to do this to my hands and feet, but you can do this to any part of your body from which you wish to creatively express yourself.

- **Creating with water:** A practice I like is intuitively painting with watercolors, letting the pigments and water guide my hand throughout the process. I'll grab a sheet of paper, or whatever medium I feel called to use, and I gather my brushes and watercolor paints. I like to come to this practice without any expectation or planning. Before I begin, I'll speak an incantation to my glass of water: "Water, guide my hand to create that which wishes to come forward." I then dip my brush in the water and into a color from my paint palette. I let myself form a connection with the brush, pigment, and water, paying attention to how the brush feels in my hand. I envision the water, paint, and brush as an extension of my fingers, my hand, and my arm. Once the water and pigment have taken over my entire arm, I bring the brush to paper. I do not think about it being perfect, I just allow the pigment and water to guide my hand. Sometimes, I'll do the entire painting practice with my eyes closed. When I open my eyes, I'll see an intricate design that I never could have planned on my own. I look for clues or messages from the spirit of the element. Water teaches us to let go of expectations and let truth come forward. If you do this creative practice, trust that it will reveal whatever you need to understand in the moment. Always offer gratitude to the water before pouring it out.

Fire

We are warm-bodied creatures who depend on fire to keep us alive. The sun provides us with light and warmth. Plants need the powerful fire from the sun to grow. Without fire, life would not exist on this planet. Our ancestors found a way to harness this powerful element. They passed down the knowledge of fire, how to cook with it, make drawings from the ashes, and unite the tribes in dances and storytelling.

Fire is essential, not only for the health of our bodies, but for our environment. Fire cooks and heats our food, allowing us to eat a wider variety of nutrients. We are fire in physical form, carrying heat in our bodies. Our stomachs are full of acid that digests our food. Certain tree seeds need fire so they can explode and become fertile. Fire clears dead brush and provides space for new life to grow. Without this life-sustaining element, we would not exist.

·

ANCESTRAL WISDOM OF FIRE

Fire is an ancestral element; an ancient power that makes all life possible. Humans are forged from a fire that has existed for millions of years. This element inspired prehistoric amphibians to grow legs and crawl out of the ocean. It guides creatures out of their dens to hunt for food, which grows toward the fire of the sun. The element of fire has the power to nurture or destroy and must be respected.

Fire allowed our ancestors to evolve. Ancient people realized that taming fire had many benefits. It allowed them to cook foods, expanding their diet and creative culinary possibilities. In the winter months, fire kept them warm. It warded off predatory animals to keep them safe, and provided light at nighttime for gathering and sharing stories. We owe gratitude to our ancestors for harnessing the great sacred flames of the volcanoes, lightning, and sun. It is for this reason that many cultures celebrate fire. This element, which has creative and destructive potential, has much to teach us.

CREATIVE TEACHINGS OF FIRE

Fire is an honest element. It is not here to sugarcoat the truth. It is purifying and transformative, burning what doesn't serve us and revealing what does. It will burn us if we do not properly respect it. But it can also heal us. The flame represents passion, rage, and epiphany.

We need fire to help us creatively express ourselves and find the imprint of who we are. Fire represents our passions, without which we become careless, unmotivated, and lost. We can use fire to explore the things that ignite our creativity. By cultivating fire practices, you can harness the righteous rage within you that burns when we are faced with injustice. It is a powerful element that burns to shine light in the darkness.

CREATIVE PRACTICES WITH FIRE

A creativity practice with fire will help you understand what you are passionate about. This can be hard for many of us when we find ourselves constantly influenced by outside noise. To activate our creativity, we must come back to the original source of creation, placing it in the center of all that we do. Here are a few ways to work with fire that can influence your creative practices. Please do these practices with caution:

- **Fire Circle:** Forming a fire circle is a great way to guide our passion and lead us to our creativity. I like to gather materials or tools that speak to my creativity. This can be any number of items. What matters is that you are present and connected to the items. I like to bunch two to three candles together and light them to intensify the flame (though you can most certainly do this with an outdoor fire if that is accessible). I create a circle using the items I gathered and

place myself in the center of the circle. While in the circle, I make a
connection with the flame, envisioning the heat of the fire as a
beam of red light shining directly into my heart. Once I have this
vision, I let that red beam connect to the item on my right. Then I
allow the red beam to go around the circle clockwise, connecting to
each item until it lands back at my heart. With each item, I ask
myself what is coming up for me. What am I feeling? How is each
tool inviting me to use it? For your practice, I invite you to spend as
much time as needed in this creative fire circle, exploring your tools
and/or your body.

- **Fire Gazing:** Fire is always speaking to us. We can tune into its
  language by gazing upon its flames. Fire is honest and does not hold
  back truth. It shows us what we need to see and burns off what we
  don't need. For this practice, I'll go somewhere I won't be disturbed. I
  light a candle (it can be either big or small) and speak into it as I am
  lighting it: "Great fire spirit, reveal to me the passion within." Then, I
  stare into the flame, noting how it flickers, how it moves, the way it
  dances. Shapes will emerge as I stare. I may see a figure dancing,
  hands opening, or a horse galloping. It does not matter if your flame is
  big or small, there is always a message in each flame. As I receive
  images from the flame, I'll envision or write about what is being
  revealed. I invite these messages to speak to me, and allow the flame
  to inform the expression of my creativity and passion. When the
  practice is complete, I offer gratitude and respect before extinguishing
  the fire.

Earth

Earth holds us throughout our lives, as we walk, grow, heal, love, and create. It
is our burial site, the place where we come home when we die. In this modern
life, many of us spend our entire lives disconnected from the earth. But when

we reconnect with the element of earth, we experience potent healing, often helping our bodies cure illnesses, negative thoughts, and stress.

By connecting to earth, we connect to ourselves and thus to our own creative abilities. We are all earthly beings. Our ancestors knew the power of healing and growth in the soil. They lived by the rhythms of Earth, eating and living seasonally. It is our solace, our place to find clarity, inspiration, and stability. It is also the place where we come to reconnect with our ancestors as it is Earth's soil that holds the bones, energy, and memories of all that has ever lived here.

*

ANCESTRAL WISDOM OF EARTH

Earth is the all-encompassing material of every living organism, including ourselves. Without earth, we would not be possible. It is no surprise that many people find peace or grounding in nature. Underneath our feet is a vast, magical wonderland of life, nutrients, history, and potential. From the earth, flowers dance in the breeze. Bison and cows graze from its grass. Corn, tomatoes, and other fresh fruits and vegetables crop up from the soil to sustain us. Stones form riverbanks, providing pathways for water to flow to different areas in a harmonious exchange. Nothing is wasted. Earth transforms and renews everything in its care, turning the deceased into life-sustaining compost. It fuels us with its energy.

Earth shows us the importance of cycles. It reminds us that there is no death, only continuation. Everything in nature returns to the soil to be used repeatedly in a never-ending cycle of life. We are a part of this cycle, this ecosystem. Our ancestors lived by this understanding, which is why they strived to protect and preserve the earth. They knew that we should not hurt or pollute it, because it is one with us, and we will be one with it again when we return to the soil to nourish new roots of possibility.

CREATIVE TEACHINGS OF EARTH

Earth teaches us the importance of rooting ourselves in everything we choose to do. Many of us spend our entire lives searching for meaning and vitality, yet it is right beneath our feet. Earth supports us in our creative endeavors, providing a ground from which we can leap to reach our dreams. Earth never apologizes for what it grows. It teaches us that we can grow stable from strong roots, we can push against the ground when we fall, and we can plant seeds of creativity in the rich soil.

Every living thing relies on the earth. When we are disconnected from the earth, we become disconnected from our bodies, which separates us from our creativity. When we are grounded and rooted to the soil under our feet, we remember ancient secrets, and we remember that we are one with all that is or ever was on this planet.

CREATIVE PRACTICES WITH EARTH

We can connect with earth to practice rooting and grounding ourselves in our truth, allowing us to embrace the instinctual nature of our bodies. We must first learn to listen before we can create. Here are ways that you can ground yourself when building a creative practice:

- **Forest shower:** Forest showers are practiced in many parts of the world. They are a wonderful way to help the body de-stress and feel at peace. It is one of my favorite practices and doesn't require much effort to reap the benefits. A forest shower isn't like the ones we take in our bathrooms. Rather, it's a practice of going outdoors and intentionally placing materials from nature on the skin, such as foliage, branches, grass, soil, and so on. I start by walking around for about ten to fifteen minutes before gathering anything that I feel called to place on my skin. Once I have a sense of the energy around me, I'll start gathering items, such as rocks, foliage, twigs, or anything that carries an energy I wish to embody. Please be sure to pick items that are safe to come in contact with your body. If you are gathering any sort of leaf or plant, make sure to properly research it before placing it on your skin.

My favorite way of connecting to the items I've gathered is by finding a place in the forest or park where I can be in solitude. I begin by placing one item at a time on the parts of my body that need grounding. Then I imagine a green root growing from the item down through my skin. I allow the root to continue down until it reaches my bone or muscle tissue. I let a green light radiate over the entire area, cleansing all my stress and aligning my body with earth energy. Feel free to explore each item you've gathered one at a time, connecting it to different parts of your body. You may also choose to put all of the items at once on your body, letting them work their grounding energy together. After my forest shower, I instantly feel inspired and full of creativity.

Encantar Reflection

Like my *abuela*, we are all creatures led by our own *instincto*. Using the elements of nature, we can tune into our instinct and creativity to understand, explore, communicate, and thrive in rhythm with the elements. It is not enough to live our lives trudging through our responsibilities and obligations. We must also consciously attune ourselves to nature, remembering the gift that is life. Our human bodies are a manifestation of the creativity of Madre Tierra. We must never disrespect her by losing touch with our creativity or with ourselves. May you live a life so rich that one day, when your hands are wrinkled and aging, you can point to your life and shout, "Look at me! Look at all that I've done! Look at all that I've created and held!" In that moment, may you rest in peaceful assurance that you are an enchanted part of all that is or ever was.

Y *así es* (and so it is).

Encantar Ritual

·

ELEMENTAL ART ALTAR

Altars are a great way to honor ourselves, our guides, our ancestors, and our sacred practices. Creativity is a sacred practice that deserves to be treated with respect. It is a great honor to creatively express ourselves, as it is the fundamental guide in experiencing our humanity. We can honor life and all that is connected to it by building an altar to show our appreciation to the spirit of creativity and all of the elements that make our existence possible.

Creating an elemental art altar combines all the elements—air, water, fire, and earth—with the tools we use in our creative practices. Next I will show you how to set up an elemental art altar. Feel free to switch out tools and items as many times as you want.

- Gather one item from each element. This can look like the following:

    Air—feather, floating seed, written poem, or incantation

    Water—seashell, fishbone, seaweed, a cup of water

    Fire—candle, incense stick, dried herbs

    Earth—rock, soil, sand, root

- Dedicate a sacred space in your home for your altar. Select a surface you'd like to use and clean it with all four elements. You may also

I invite creativity to enchant me so I may always
find myself and fully harness the power of my spirit.

cleanse it with just one element, it is completely up to you. You can use water to wipe down the area, burn incense and let the smoke cleanse the area, use air by speaking an incantation directly to the altar, and earth by throwing a bit of soil onto the surface.

- Begin by intuitively placing all the elements you gathered on your altar. This does not have to look any certain way, just do what feels right to you.
- Gather the tools and items with which you wish to adorn your elemental art altar. This can be a journal if you wish to honor your writing, paint brushes if you wish to honor your painting, or a musical instrument if you wish to honor your musical gifts, whatever you like. Feel free to swap out tools and items as needed.
- Go to your elemental art altar daily and speak words of appreciation to the spirit of creativity. Treat it as you would an ancestral altar, or spirit guide altar. Creativity is the spirit of humanity, and in this format you are honoring yourself through this altar.
- Repeat this phrase to complete your elemental altar ritual:

Y *así es* (and so it is).

conjurar

Offering Six

Conjurar
(Conjure)

Incantation

I will not let my pain dictate who I am. My painful experiences speak to what I've survived, not how I must live. I am capable of creating strength and wisdom from my experiences and forgive that which has made me feel fear. I forgive to know what it means to feel peace. I forgive because I know I deserve to live by the truth of my imprint.

Shortened Incantation

I am the conjurer of strength, transmuting and shape-shifting everything that ails me and everything that pains me. I transmute my painful experiences to opportunities of growth and expansion.

Conjurar,
Una Fabúla

A young woman was walking through the forest when she came across an emerald. It sparkled in the sunlight, beckoning the woman to it. Moss had grown around the emerald. The weight of the gem pushed it down into the earth. The woman tried to pick up the emerald, but she wasn't strong enough to pull it free from the earth. She heaved and panted, pushing and pulling at the gem, but it was no use. Exhausted, she sat next to the gem and made a wish under her breath.

"I wish for strength," she whispered.

Out of the ground emerged a *diosa* (goddess). She carried a long needle in her bronze hand. Before the girl could ask who she was, the *diosa* stabbed her in the heart with the needle. The woman winced in pain.

"Why did you do this? It hurts!" the woman cried.

The *diosa* stooped down in front of the woman, inviting her to face her and stare into her eyes. "You asked for strength," the *diosa* said. "Strength is my sister. But you can't meet her until you've felt the sharp sting of my needle and looked into my eyes."

"Why? Who are you?" the woman pleaded.

"I am the Diosa of Pain."

The woman, who'd been squinting in agony, softened her gaze and focused on the Diosa of Pain's eyes. The *diosa* smiled, stood, and walked back into the ground. The woman turned and tried again to remove the emerald from the earth. It still would not budge.

"I don't understand. I stared pain in the eyes. Where is the strength?"

Suddenly, a *diosa* swooped down from the tree canopy and wrapped her dark green cloak around the woman's entire body. The cloak was a heavy, almost unbearable weight. It suffocated the woman as she tried to free herself. With each movement, the pain in her heart bled and ached.

"Why are you smothering me? Who are you?" The woman wheezed.

"I am the Diosa of Grief." A voice spoke into the cloak. Pain and Strength are my sisters. If you want to know strength, you must face Pain and move through Grief."

"I cannot move!" the woman shouted.

"And you will not be able to move. Not until you sit with me, accept my weight, and surrender to my cloak," Grief replied.

The pain in the woman's chest burned through her entire body. She tried to move away from it, but the pain grew stronger with every attempt. She tried bargaining with the *diosa*.

"If you let me out, I'll show you where to find a lovely emerald."

Diosa of Grief remained silent. The woman pleaded with the *diosa* to let her go. She screamed with rage, clawing at the cloak, trying to rip it to shreds. The cloak was too heavy and thick. After hours of wrestling with the cloak, the woman fell into herself and wept. As the tears fell, the blood from her heart began to dry. With each sob, her wound healed, leaving a thick, tender scar. She leaned on the cloak, using its velvety fabric to wipe her tears. Eventually, she fell asleep in the embrace of the cloak. When she awoke, the Diosa of Grief and her cloak were gone.

The woman leapt to her feet. She spun around, looking for the Diosa of Strength. But nobody appeared. Then she heard a faint voice.

"I am here," the voice beckoned.

The woman followed the voice down the hill to the lake.

"Where? I do not see you."

"Come closer." The voice called.

The voice seemed to be coming from the lake. The girl ran to the edge of the water and looked across the lake.

"Here," the voice called from below.

The girl looked down at the water and saw her own reflection. Her appearance was different. Her posture and physique had changed. She looked like a *diosa*. Pain and Grief appeared beside her.

"You are our sister, the Diosa of Strength," they said in unison.

The woman took a breath, thanked her sisters, and returned to the emerald. She easily plucked it from the dirt and broke it in half, giving a piece to each of her sisters.

"Don't you want to keep a piece for yourself?" they asked.

The woman pointed to the place on her chest where the scar used to be. The wound had transformed into a brilliant emerald.

In 2008 on a hot July summer night, I rode in the back of a police car, dazed and silent. I still remember the sharp, cold interior, the smell of metal, the essence of hopelessness lingering in the back of that car. My body couldn't stop shivering, still trying to process what I'd just experienced. The policeman touched my shoulder, jolting me from my state of shock. I looked up and realized we were at my parents' house, where I still lived. Amá opened the door and immediately noticed my red bruised neck. Her warm arms wrapped my cold body in a hug, like a blanket I never wanted to take off. Apá came rushing to the door, and the policeman explained the incident. I still remember the words that rolled off the policeman's tongue. It was a phrase he'd grown accustomed to saying. *"Your daughter has been a victim of battery."* The words *victim* and *battery* shot into my brain, pinballing off the inner walls of my skull, through my bruised neck, and down into my entire body.

Physical abuse was a familiar evil in my childhood environment. I've seen dragons unleash themselves through the bodies of people I'd once trusted to keep me safe. Loving hands suddenly morphed into fists of fury. Some of my family members seemed eager to paint their partners with bruises. It became commonplace, specifically toward the women in my family. When I first witnessed physical abuse at age twelve, I swore I'd never let that happen to me. I vowed to never allow myself to be in a situation where someone could hurt me that way. Of course, I wasn't aware that some dragons are masters at disguising themselves until the moment they strike.

Every minute of every day, nearly twenty people are physically abused by an intimate partner in the United States.[3] One in four women and one in nine men experience intimate partner abuse.[4] The statistics are even worse for someone who is part of the LGBTQIA2S+ community. Overall, more than 10 million people in one year will experience domestic violence. Every minute, as we brush our teeth, drink our coffee, or comb our hair, someone is being physically abused. It is a shocking reality that, in many households, has become a common occurrence.

Some of us are told to "get over" abuse. We're told "it's not that bad." So, we retreat into ourselves, imploding from the weight of the unacknowledged trauma. Some of us become prisoners in isolation, confusion, and fear. The moment I heard the cop tell my parents, "Your daughter has been a victim of battery," I melded with those words. It was as if those words suddenly became everything that I'd ever known about myself. I was a stranger to myself—a victim. For a long time, I didn't know how to emancipate myself from victimhood. I smothered myself with quotes of strength, painting over my open wounds, thinking this is what it looks like to overcome abuse. I did not realize how desperately I was trying to survive.

After that night, I did what a lot of abuse survivors do. I tried to move on, move forward, move away from the experience. I thought I could keep the trauma at bay by not talking about what happened to me. I kept myself busy, constantly jumping from task to task, always running two steps ahead of the pain. I internalized my suffering into such a deep cavern, it festered, turning into anger and self-sabotaging thoughts. I did everything I could think of to be "strong."

But what I thought was strength was actually avoidance. Later, I learned that barricading myself inside tall walls of empowering quotes and busying myself with daily tasks were clever ways of hiding from the pain I couldn't bear to face.

One of my favorite words in Spanish, one that I've built a personal relationship with through my emancipation from victimhood, is *desahogar* (vent). Though this term translates to *vent*, it can be also interpreted as *undrown*. This word is common in many Latine/x households that understand the sacred practice of venting and how it can help with coping and healing. For me, strength is *desahogar*. It is releasing everything that needs to be said and feeling everything that needs to be felt, so we don't drown in the deep, dark abyss of our painful thoughts and feelings. With the practice of *desahogar*, we conjure our imprint, bringing it forth to heal what needs healing.

I believe that as inhabitants of Madre Tierra, we all carry the potential of growth and expansion. Some moments will be filled with pure enjoyment, opportunities to expand our curiosity and leap at the thrill of being alive. Other experiences will bring us to our knees in pain, grief, and devastation, requiring all our attention and energy to recover. We must never let these experiences dim our magic. Instead, we must embrace these moments with the eyes of the *brujx/e*. The *brujx/e* has the ability to transform all that ails us into powerful forces of reclamation and healing. We must tap into our potential to create healing from pain, growth from sadness, and strength from loss. We are conjurers of our own magic, liberating ourselves out of victimhood and into healing and forgiveness. We start our conjuring practice by understanding that we can turn our victim into a victor.

Conjurar Embodiment Exercise: Our Most Powerful Selves

In this visualization exercise, we will embody our most powerful selves. Empowerment comes from a space of unshakable confidence. Come to this exercise whenever you need to conjure your power.

ADORNING OUR BODIES (OPTIONAL)

Before the visualization journey of this exercise, I invite you to dress in clothing that makes you feel powerful. For me, indigenous clothing that connects me to my culture makes me feel empowered. But it may also look like business attire, provocative apparel, or fine fabrics. You may also choose to adorn your body with empowering accessories or makeup. If doing this isn't accessible to you, feel free to envision your clothing.

VISUALIZATION JOURNEY

- Sit comfortably in a chair and close your eyes. Allow the empowering clothing you are wearing to magnify your confidence. Notice how the confidence feels as it moves through your body. How does your body respond? It may respond by straightening your back and raising your chin to the sky.
- Envision the chair you are sitting on as a throne. Allow your mind to build its own image of how the throne looks and feels. Allow the images of your throne to build and become more detailed. How does your body feel, sitting on this throne? Take a memory snapshot in your mind and come back to this image of your most empowered self when you feel you need this energy.
- When you have a strong image in your mind of you on your throne, I invite you to draw it in the box on the next page. If drawing isn't something you are comfortable with, feel free to journal your experience, writing about how you look and feel. You may choose to hang up your words or drawing in a place where you can easily see it and embody your empowerment every day.

A Victim of Your Own Suffering

When I was declared a victim on that July summer night, I fully believed every letter of my new identity. My inner victim showed up in every aspect of my life, my body, and my experiences. My anger burned hot in my body, turning into inflammation that affected my health. I harbored severe limiting beliefs and would sabotage myself at every turn. I was critical of my body and my decisions, which prevented me from living fully. Being aligned with victimhood took me out of alignment with my imprint, the spirit of my empowered self. The pain from the misalignment with our imprint has a way of catching up to us and stopping us in our tracks. It demands our attention, whether we want to acknowledge it or not. I spent years thinking my pain was a heavy cloak that I couldn't shake, no matter how I exhausted myself trying. I was so tangled in the dark cloak of my grief, I couldn't feel or see the sun.

Survival over healing is the theme for many of us who come from marginalized communities. Some of us were never shown what it means to heal. We have been raised by caregivers who've detached themselves from their own humanity to survive. In my household, conversations that carried weight, the kind of weight that makes you sink in your seat, were usually avoided. It wasn't normal for us to talk about our feelings. This is true for many Latine/x households. I saw Amá hold back her heart countless times because she didn't know how to express what she was feeling. Many of our guardians and parents grew up drowning their imprint in inherited generational patterns, not realizing they would also be drowning their own children. This is a generational pattern derived from internalized oppression. But our bodies know how to heal, integrate, and recover, if we give them the freedom to do so.

It is important to understand that we cannot control everything that happens, but we can control how we respond to what's happened. Even though I was a victim of physical abuse, I learned that I could choose not to stay in victimhood. This realization changed everything for me.

Decolonize Your Healing

No matter what hardships we may experience, healing is possible. But it is important to understand that healing is not a linear path. It requires us to meet ourselves with patience and grace. While I never wish any pain upon anyone, I believe that pain and grief can be some of the most transformative feelings we can experience. I like to think that pain and grief are the sisters of strength, they rely on one another for their existence, joined at the root. Strength is our protective barrier, it is how we become sorcerers—the true conjurers of our own story. We must conjure strength from the deep place of wisdom in our imprint, not from a place influenced by external sources.

Before colonialism, healing was done by medicine people who were gifted and trained to cure ailments of the body, mind, and spirit. Thanks to the storytellers and medicine people who survived colonialism, some of those sacred practices are still alive today. Though Western medicine is our predominant path to healing in modern society, it is not the only way. Healing is a multifaceted practice that may be a departure from what you witnessed growing up. Before I knew what healing the self was, I unconsciously picked up healing patterns from my family. I coped in ways that I'd seen Amá or Abuela cope. Many of those coping strategies did more damage than good. Some did nothing at all. At times, healing means unlearning the harmful coping strategies embedded in us during childhood. To embark on the path of healing according to our individual needs, we must decolonize and redefine what healing means for us.

Decolonial work is everyone's work, not just that of Black, Brown, and Indigenous peoples reclaiming traditions that were taken from us. We all must do the work of decolonizing every practice we've been steeped in and ask ourselves if these ways embrace the imprint of who we are. We must ask ourselves, "Does this view or practice honor me in every way possible? Does it exclude my goals, dreams, or opinions? Is it harmful to my body or spirit?" Decolonizing our healing is revolutionary work that sets all of us free from societal expectations, victimhood, generational trauma, internalized oppression, and pain—because decolonizing is reclamation and liberation in action.

I began decolonizing my healing when I stopped burying my pain. It was excruciating to feel all of that stored suffering that had been buried for so long. I realized I had bullied myself into submission, just like a colonizer. My pain never left, because I never tended to the wounds from the trauma I'd witnessed and endured. When I chose to approach my healing through a decolonized lens, I broke centuries of generational cycles.

To conjure healing, we must give ourselves the opportunity to undrown our imprint (our spirit) by speaking out about all that ails us. The act of *desahogar* gives us the opportunity to understand, process, and sit with the discomfort of difficult feelings. It is important to remind yourself that it's okay to feel discomfort, and that it won't last forever. As soon as we acknowledge the pain, it will begin to transform into strength, empowerment, and understanding.

We must come to every aching part of ourselves with love and compassion, free from judgment. We must embrace ourselves, look in the mirror, and say:

"I am strong because I carry the strength of my *abuelas*, *abuelos*, and ancestors. I am made up of every element of strength. Every cell in my body holds the power of the ocean. Every bone is solid as stone. Each breath in my lungs represents an audacious will to live. My voice wields the fierceness of fire. I conjure all the might and fortitude of my people, my home, and myself."

We may use this empowerment incantation however we see fit, by chanting it, screaming it, feeling it, singing it, or humming it. Hold the image of your empowered self on the throne in your mind as you recite this incantation. Remember that you are the sorcerer/ess/x of your life. You get to choose how to live, and what it means to heal.

What We Learn in Forgiveness

Part of decolonizing our healing is understanding true forgiveness. After I had experienced physical abuse, I was pressured by some people to forgive the person who hurt me. I found the thought to be dismissive and suffocating. How could I forgive someone who betrayed my trust and physically assaulted me? I've struggled with the concept that to find peace, we must forgive our abusers/oppressors.

I cannot tell you to forgive someone who harmed you. But I can tell you that forgiveness is almost never about those who hurt us. Forgiveness is the permission we give to ourselves to be free from the pain of the hurt someone caused. We forgive to free ourselves, no one else.

To conjure forgiveness, we must acknowledge and move through our own judgment, grief, pettiness, and resentment. Forgiveness doesn't have to be a physical conversation with the person who caused you pain. You can forgive in your own space, your own way, your own time.

Forgiveness can come in many ways:

- In *pláticas* (talks), letting yourself speak with someone or with yourself about the pain you experienced.
- In reclamation, by taking back what was stolen from you, such as your sense of safety, self-worth, or joy.
- In intent, by smiling, not because you were told "you look prettier when you smile," but because you are granting yourself full permission to bask in joy rather than pain.
- In peace, by waking up every day and choosing stillness rather than chaos.

As a conjurer of your own forgiveness, you may discover that you need to forgive yourself, as well. The parts of you that are judgmental, stuck in victimhood, angrily lashing out, or reactive all developed to protect you. When you meet those parts with gratitude and forgiveness, you will transform your reactions to the trauma. Those victim parts within will relax and find new, healthier ways of helping you, leading you into the truth of your imprint.

Conjurar Practice

DESAHOGAR (UNDROWN)

In *curanderismo*—a Latin American folk healing practice that uses the mind, body, and spirit to heal, there is an important element called *pláticas* (talks). In the process of *curanderismo*, also known as *curanderas, curanderos,* or *curanderxs*, the practice of *desahogar* (vent) is used to undrown the body and spirit from whatever ails it. This sacred practice helps those who need a safe space to speak of their pains with someone who specializes in the workings of *curanderismo*. The idea is that, when the body is drowning, words help it float.

Speaking about what pains us is a gateway to understanding how we can help ourselves heal. Many of us have silenced our words and buried our pains because society has taught us that silence means strength. But as we move into a space of healing generational traumas, internalized oppression, victimization, and decolonization, *pláticas* can liberate us from familial and societal conditioning.

Though this sacred practice is usually done with someone skilled in *curanderismo*, you may undrown yourself through heartfelt conversations. If having a *plática* with a skilled *curandero/a/x* isn't accessible to you, I invite you to do the following practice instead:

• Seek out a trusted friend with whom you'd like to share this *plática*. Let your friend know you wish to unburden yourself through a heartfelt conversation and ask if your friend has the mental and spiritual space to hear you. (If speaking with someone physically isn't an option, I invite you to replace the "friend" in this exercise with your journal. You can unburden yourself in your journal as if it were a trusted friend.) Keep in mind that this *plática* has no strict rules for how it must go. This is an intuitive conversation in which the purpose is to undrown your spirit by speaking out about what is causing you pain.

- Allow yourself to open up to your friend. Share with this person whatever has been laying heavy on your heart and why. Continue to speak about all that ails you. Do not hold back.

- As you unburden yourself, visualize your spirit undrowning itself by rising from the deep waters of suffering, floating to the surface to breathe.

- Take deep breaths, allowing your lungs to be filled with air in between this *plática* so you can feel the benefits of this heartfelt conversation.

Conjurar Journal Prompts

I invite you to create your own healing practice. Imagine all that you need to conjure to assist you in finding peace of mind, body, and spirit. Connect with your imprint, asking it to answer the following questions:

What does healing look like for me?

What can I do right now that would give me peace of mind, body, and spirit?

_____

_____

_____

_____

How can I be an active participant in my healing in a way that feels safe and inclusive to my blessed imprint?

_____

_____

_____

_____

What forces can I conjure to assist me in my healing? My ancestors? Elements of nature? Guides and spirits?

_____

_____

_____

_____

Follow the wisdom of your imprint, allowing it to take you through your healing process, conjuring all the support you need as you go. You may come back to these journal prompts as often as needed, changing them to fit your needs.

Conjurar Reflection

Every day is an opportunity for growth, and every painful experience is an opportunity for wisdom. It is okay to say: "Yes, I experienced suffering. I was a victim of this situation, but I choose not to align myself with victimhood." Victimhood can lead to internalized oppression if we identify with it for too long. It is vital that we center our healing in decolonizing our recovery from trauma. Before colonialism, genocide, and erasure, our ancestors and the ancients that walked before us held the wisdom of healing. We have access to that wisdom. By being active participants in processing our pain, finding forgiveness, and healing through a decolonized lens, we remove the barriers of our spirit. May you see pain as an invitation to healing, forgiveness, and strength. May you become the conjurer of all the benevolent powers waiting to assist you, and may you turn traumatic experiences into magical opportunities for healing sorcery.

Conjurar Poetry Spell Ritual

"A STANZA A DAY KEEPS THE HEARTACHE AT BAY"

You don't need to be a writer to be a poet. We are all born poets. Poetry is an extension of our humanness and, lucky for you, you are human! When processing our pain, poetry can be a helpful ritual. Sometimes, our pain is best healed through the dance of words. (Please note that for this ritual, you will travel into a space that could be a trigger for you. If you are not ready right now, that's okay. You may skip this ritual and come back to it when you feel comfortable.)

I am the conjurer of strength, transmuting and
shapeshifting everything that ails me and everything that
pains me. I transmute my painful experiences to
opportunities of growth and expansion.

This ritual is *desahogar* (vent or undrown) in poetry form. You will travel to a painful memory that is holding you back. Using the tool of poetry, you will make medicine out of that moment. You will write five stanzas with two lines each. (A stanza is a group of lines that are arranged together in a recurring pattern, forming a poem). The full poem will be ten lines. This is not by accident. The number ten represents new beginnings, completeness, and possibilities. We are intentionally writing ten lines to amplify the spell and bring forth a new beginning energy.

To do this ritual:

- Grab a notebook or piece of paper and something to write with.
- Find a space where you feel safe and get comfortable.
- I find it's helpful to bring something that makes you feel safe. This can be a picture of an ancestor, a candle, burning your favorite herbal blend, a deity statue, or anything that symbolizes protection for you. I find this helpful, because when we travel back to a triggering memory, being surrounded by items and energies that help us feel safe is important.
- When you are ready, close your eyes and think about something you had to overcome that you still carry with you today.
- Once you have that memory, grab your paper and formulate your stanzas. Each line or stanza may be as long or as short as you'd like. Write your stanzas using this guide:

> First line: What did this experience make you believe about yourself?
>
> Second line: What is the truth about yourself?
>
> *Space*
>
> Third line: How did this experience shame you?

Fourth line: How can you transform that shame into light?

Space

Fifth line: How has this experience victimized you?

Sixth line: How has this experience called you to explore your strength?

Space

Seventh line: What do you feel this experience took from you?

Eighth line: How can you reclaim what was taken?

Space

Ninth line: What did you tell yourself after this experience?

Tenth line: What can you tell yourself now that will help you heal?

This practice helps *desahogar* (undrown) the imprint. By following each answer with another answer centered on transformation, we can transmute our experience into an opportunity for wisdom and healing. Come back to this poem as often as needed to remind yourself that you are the conjurer of your healing, strength, and forgiveness.

Y así es (and so it is).

expresión

Part Four

Expresión

(Expression)

Tengo piel gruesa y bien lo siento

My skin smells of culture y bien lo veo

I am made of spirit and bone

First a sheep, now becoming a crone

Unafraid of embracing everything I need to be

Resurrecting in between every death cycle
that has brought me to my knees

Once a low whisper in the distance

Now a sharp laugh expressing its existence

—EMBODIED

convocar

Offering Seven

Convocar
(Summon)

Incantation

I come from ancient magic as old as daylight. It runs through me like the river of blood that nourishes my bones. The history of how I came to be is a history I shall seek and praise. It is a history that reminds me why I am here, purposefully, intentionally, and with audacity.

Shortened Incantation

I embrace all that I was and all I am becoming. I welcome all that I am yet to be. I am vibrant and vibrating with the hum of becoming.

Convocar,
Una Fabúla

Coatlicue (this name translates to "Serpent Skirt" in the Aztec language of Nahuatl) is the Aztec earth goddess and mother to gods and mortals. The Aztecs believed that Coatlicue is responsible for the creation of the moon, as well as the stars and the sun. In Aztec mythology, Coatlicue was a priestess who was responsible for the care of a legendary mountaintop named Coatepec (Snake Mountain, also spelled Coatepetl). One day, Coatlicue was blessing the holy shrine at the top of the mountain when a ball of white feathers suddenly fell from the sky. Coatlicue grabbed the ball of white feathers and tucked it into her belt. She then miraculously became pregnant with the Aztec sun and war god, Huitzilopochtli. Coatlicue's children were enraged at their mother's pregnancy. She had no husband at the time, so they viewed it as dishonorable. Her children attempted to kill her, but Huitzilopochtli came bursting from her womb, fully grown and ready to defend his mother. Huitzilopochtli killed his sister Coyolxauhqui and threw her head into the sky, where the Aztecs believed it became the moon. He also killed his four hundred brothers, called the Centzon Huitznahua. According to Aztec legend, they became the stars.

As a child, I liked to sit quietly, listening to the family chatter among grown-ups. They loved to share their "back at home" stories. I saw the faces of my family light up as they traced back through treasured memories. They brought out boxes of fragile, ripped photos, pictures of people and neighborhoods I didn't recognize. Amá would show me a photo and say *"Mira, esta soy yo allí en mi pueblo"* (Look, this is me, there in my town). It was an image of my mother as a little girl with short, messy curls and a wide grin. The girl stood in front of scattered bushes and trees, wearing an embroidered top and tattered shorts. In the corner of the photograph, I could just make out the foot of a chicken. The photo was in black and white with folded and creased edges. Amá stared into the picture as if she were trying to remember every detail of that moment. I wondered if maybe this is how we hold on to memories we're afraid to lose—we bring out old boxes of worn photos and summon the past back to life.

"Back at home" meant back in Mexico, the home to our many *tios, tias, primos, abuelas y abuelos*. Although we lived in the United States, *mi familia* loved to reminisce about their days in Mexico. All of their faded memories came to life as they spoke.

"Allá en mi pueblo" (There in my town), Amá would start in Spanish as she pulled photos from the old box, "I would sell chicken eggs so I could buy a piece of *pan dulce* (sweet bread). I love *pan dulce*! I would go from door to door with my basket of eggs, selling them to all of my neighbors. As soon as I had

enough money, I would run to the bakery to get my piece of *pan*. I didn't mind waking up extra early to collect chicken eggs if it meant I could eat delicious *pan dulce!*"

Then, from across the dinner table, Apá would follow in Spanish: "Back at home, my grandmother made the spiciest menudo every Sunday morning. My favorite thing to do was dip my *bolillo* (bread roll) into the *caldito* (broth) and take a big bite. There is something about eating menudo in your grandmother's house back in Mexico. It is something you can never forget. I miss her menudo so much, but I especially miss her."

I listened as my parents, uncles, and aunts would go around the dinner table, each sharing a memory from back at home, eagerly summoning spirits from the past.

As a young girl, I listened to these stories with curiosity, but never realized their significance. My family's "back at home" stories taught me the importance of listening with intention to fully grasp what was being shared. As a child of Mexican immigrant parents who came to the United States, the place where I was born, I had the experience of living in two worlds. One world was that of my parents, the origin of our culture—a diaspora of traditions, beliefs, foods, and language. The other world, where I was born, was a strange land of forced assimilation for anyone who wasn't Caucasian. While living in two worlds, I felt strong pressure by normalized society to forget my own roots. Many immigrant families are told there isn't enough room to be from both worlds, so we must choose. We feel we must hide our heritage to exist and fit into this society. So, we detach ourselves from what is deemed "unimportant" about us. For some, survival means forgetting the origins of our history, and the history of those who came before us.

If we wish to understand where we are going, we must first understand where we come from. The reason many of us struggle to see a path in front of us is because we need to reconnect with the history of our ancestors, our lineages, our stories. Back at home stories are vital pathways to self-discovery. Oppressive leaders know the power of history, of our stories. That's why books that speak the truth about the history of colonialism, genocide, and erasure are being banned from public spaces today. They know that when we summon the power of our history, we can no longer be manipulated into submission.

We must give ourselves full permission to voyage through the roots growing from the soles of our feet. We must learn why *abuelas y abuelos* stare off into the horizon, as if recollecting parts of themselves. We must listen with intent to the "back at home" stories of our *amás* and *apás* and look through the old boxes of faded, ripped photos with them. Our ancestors and elders likely never wanted us to assimilate and lose touch with our history. Our parents, just like us, had to assimilate in a new country to survive. They were never given the option to live freely in their culture, language, and traditions. And still, they found these beautiful ways of sharing our history, through old photographs and stories. One day, it will be up to us to pass down the "back at home" stories, so listen and learn, dear friend.

This chapter isn't a history lesson, it is an invitation for you to discover and summon the roots of your imprint. Summon, because these roots have always been there, and they are never fully gone. Summoning is different than conjuring. Here, we are bringing a powerful force to life within ourselves. Summoning is calling forth the ancient magic that has always been a part of us. When we conjure, the way we did in Offering Six, we are pulling attributes from people, places, and things that inspire us. When we summon, we are calling on people from our past, ancient spirits, or our guides. Though some of us may think we are reconnecting with our history and cultural roots for the first time, the truth is that history has always been with us. We are just now activating the remembrance of it within us. When we allow ourselves to voyage through the magical and painful portals of our history, we will see many missing pieces slowly come back together, mending themselves with truth, care, and love. We'll start with the simplest of acts, tuning in, slowing down, and listening.

Convocar Embodiment Exercise: Summon through Your Senses

Passive listening is different than listening with intent. Intentional listening means you take what is being shared into your bones, your soul, allowing it to alchemize with your being. In this exercise, I will guide you through an embodiment journey that will show you how to intentionally listen with all of your senses. It is our senses that guide our understanding. This is a powerful teaching that will help you summon the magic of your history, old family legends, and ancestral gifts that live within you.

- I invite you to lie down and close your eyes for this exercise. Set an intention before starting your visualization. Call to mind the outcome you wish to receive from this journey.
- Take a deep breath—inhale through your nose and exhale through your mouth. Rest your hands on your chest.
- Bring your awareness to your senses. Allow your senses of hearing, sight, taste, smell, and touch to become fully immersed in the present moment. Give your senses permission to become fully alive.
- Let your eyes seek out shapes or colors on the insides of your eyelids. What do you see?
- Let your ears listen deeply for ancient voices and pull them into your body, filling up your chest and stomach. What are they saying?
- Pay attention to the flavors swirling in your mouth. What do they taste like?
- Allow ancient, fragrant smells to take hold of your nose. What aromas are floating through your being right now?
- Let your hands move over your body to feel the places where your senses are coming alive. What does it feel like? Each sense is revealing an ancient wisdom of history, legends, and ancestral gifts for you to receive.

- Envision yourself on a voyage through the rich ancient lands of your ancestors. As you move through these lands, intentionally listen, touch, smell, taste, see, and take in all that is around you.
- Invite your ancestors to show you around. Ask them what they wish for you to know. Bring forth their wisdom, allowing it to circulate through you as you continue your path.
- Stay in this place of ancestral connection for as long as you like. When you are ready, you may open your eyes, wiggle your toes and fingers to ground your body, and journal about all you experienced on your journey.

Y *así es* (and so it is).

Elders over Assimilation

Apá pulled an old picture from the box on our kitchen table. It was a photo of Great-Grandmother Socorro in front of the border between Juarez, Mexico, and El Paso, Texas. Great-Grandmother Socorro wore a lace veil that covered her head and was draped across her shoulders. Her dress hugged her sturdy body, reaching just below her knees. Abuela was only five-foot-one but had a robust presence. Behind her was a busy background with Spanish signs that read, "*Bienvenidos a Mexico*" (Welcome to Mexico), and dirt roads lined with cars.

Apá looked at the image for a long time and finally said in Spanish: "You know, I was going to be a famous soccer player. I was very good at soccer. They gave me an opportunity to audition for a famous league from my hometown, Santos Laguna, to be on the Mexican professional soccer team that competes in the Liga Mexico. I never made it to my audition, because that day my *abuela* passed to the afterlife." Apá smiled from the corner of his mouth, and his eyes became cloudy with tears. "*La extraño mucho a mi abuela*" (I miss my grand-mother so much), he said. "*Después de su muerte, tu mamá y yo nos enamora-mos y unos años después tuvimos a ti, y a tus hermanas y hermano*" (After her death, your mother and I fell in love, and a few years later we had you and your sisters and brother).

As Apá shared his story about the day Great-Grandmother Socorro passed to the afterlife, I could see how our family's stories affect our destinies in profound ways that reach beyond historical context. We are woven into every breath, every voyage, every story, and every memory of our elders. Each step our elders took led them toward our creation, toward how they came to hold us in their arms for the first time. Had Apá gone to that soccer audition, I don't know if I would be here today. After Great-Grandmother Socorro's death, Apá never auditioned. He stayed in his hometown, met Amá, and the rest is history—my history.

My elders are my *tios, tias, abuelas*, and my parents. But your elders don't have to be blood related. They can be anyone who holds stories of your history, the history that led to your creation. Because some of these individuals may not be accessible to us, the story of our history isn't solely told by family members. Our history can also be sought by reclaiming our cultural roots. We may absorb our history by leaning into our listening and seeking knowledge through the roots that grow from the soles of our feet, which ultimately connect us to all that ever was.

I didn't grow up embracing my cultural roots, because I was guided as a child to assimilate to white "American" culture. I put "America" in quotations because Latin American countries are also America, but the United States has centered itself on this vast continent. When I discovered poetry, I discovered what it meant to reclaim my stories and, thus, my cultural roots. I would spend hours reading books by Sandra Cisneros, Dr. Clarissa Pinkola Estés, and Gloria Evangelina Anzaldúa, among others. Each of their teachings guided me to see the importance of our family and cultural history. They taught me to summon the magic inside of me to help me remember, to help me heal. When I summoned my magic, I discovered the power of culture, the power of the stories, of where we come from, and the elders that brought us to this life.

Leaning into our listening is how we summon the strength and magic of our history and cultural roots. This can be done both on a physical and intuitive plane. As we have previously discussed, the body is a portal to our imprint, and our imprint is an extension of our cultural roots. Through the sacred practice of summoning, we can communicate with our ancestors who have departed from this Earth, like my Great-Grandmother Socorro. Even if you have little or no background information on your cultural traditions, I believe the body can make connections intuitively, because our DNA remembers the historical information of our bloodlines.

Convocar Practice

SUMMONING THE POWER OF YOUR CULTURAL ROOTS

Here are some of my favorite ways to intuitively connect to cultural roots:

- Dance and listen to songs from your culture. I choose to listen to music in the native language of my ancestors. Even if I may not always understand what they are saying, listening to the words and sounds, and connecting to the vibration of the music opens a pathway between my body and my cultural roots.
- Eat, cook, and learn recipes from your culture. Cooking and sharing meals together create bonds that reconnect us to our roots. By eating the traditional foods of our culture, foods that nourished the bodies of our ancestors, we awaken a remembering in our own bodies.
- If you are a gardener or farmer, growing foods that are traditional to your culture is also a great way to bond with your elders. For me, growing foods

that I know my *abuela* has grown allows me to feel closer to her. It literally connects me to the roots of my past. (I share a ritual at the end of this chapter on this.)

- Dress in traditional clothes from your culture. Dressing in traditional clothing allows me to deepen my connection to my heritage. I feel proud, centered, and guided when I am wearing clothing that my ancestors wore.

The most important thing to remember in cultural summoning practices is to pay attention to how your body feels while eating, cooking, or growing your cultural foods. How alive does your imprint feel while dancing to songs from your cultural roots? Does your body feel beautiful and embraced by your elders when you dress in traditional clothing from your heritage? All the feelings that come up for you are essential in reconnecting you to your history.

HONORING YOUR ANCESTORS

Once we have a strong connection to our culture, we can nurture the bond through simple acts that honor our ancestors. Some of my favorite ways to honor my ancestors are the following:

- I write and communicate with my ancestors in an ancestral journal as frequently as possible. One of my favorite ways to communicate is by writing poems dedicated to each ancestor I wish to honor.
- I grow and tend to plants or flowers that I bought or planted in honor of an ancestor (or all of my ancestors in general). I tend to these plants daily, watering them, singing to them, and dancing around them as a gesture of love and respect for my ancestors.
- To honor my ancestors for whom I don't have a picture or a name, I like to envision what they looked like and imagine their names. I

enjoy painting images of my ancestors I've been unable to trace to bring their memory to life. I don't worry about making the paintings perfect. Instead, I focus on how my ancestors appear in my mind and try to paint their image. I envision what their hair color was, their features, eye colors, and so on, until I have a complete portrait.

- Building an ancestral altar with items my ancestors loved. In my lineage, we have many creative ancestors, so I like to adorn my ancestral altar with musical tools, paintbrushes, embroidery, and knitting tools. If you don't know what your ancestors loved, use the embodiment exercise mentioned previously to connect to your ancestors and ask them.

These sacred practices help us connect to the power that radiates from the bodies of our ancestors, from the earth, and up through roots from the soles of our feet. These practices are like bridges that allow us to stay in communication with our elders, ancestors, and ancient relatives, and thus stay in communication with ourselves. When we build a practice of honoring our ancestors, we are summoning the parts of ourselves that have been hidden through assimilation, abuse, and erasure. It is through the summoning of the people from our rich past that we can bring forth everything we need.

Listening with Intent

We can lean in to our listening by sitting down with the elders in our families. Many of our elders are eager to tell stories. Sadly, because of the disinterest of some of their relatives, they may fall silent. The best way to come back to yourself is to become curious. It is through curiosity that we cultivate the passion to seek, ask, learn, and become. When I became curious about my history, I no longer sat passively at the table where the fragile ripped photos were being passed around. I started asking questions about the places where the photos were taken, what the people in the photos were doing at the time, and what was happening historically around them. Before I knew it, I was holding years of someone's life in my hands, years of a powerful history that slowly paved a path to my own becoming.

If talking to family members is not an option for you, pour yourself into the history books of your ancestral lands. This is also a great way to lean in to your listening and summon stories of your cultural history. We can learn what was happening politically in our native countries and the history behind traditional practices and rituals from our culture. The history of my Mexican culture was not taught in the schools I attended in the United States. Eventually, I decided I would never let school be my only source of knowledge. These days, there are many accessible ways we can learn. There are podcasts, educational videos, library books, online resources, educators, and community events that help us summon our history. On my own listening journey, I've discovered many ancient stories that I admire, one of them being the story of the Coatlicue at the beginning of this chapter. I encourage you to find ancient stories and legends from your history, write them down, and share them.

To speak and learn from an elder who may no longer be in our earthly realm, you can lean in to your listening by performing the *Reclamar* Ritual: Ancestral Dream Visit from Offering Two. For the elders who are still with you in the physical realm, here are some prompts to ask them:

Convocar Journal Prompt:
Interviewing Your Elders

What is the story of your life?

_____

_____

_____

_____

_____

What is the story of your elders?

_____

_____

_____

_____

_____

What are some rituals and beliefs that you practice from our culture?

_____

_____

_____

_____

_____

Why are these rituals and beliefs important to you?

_____

_____

_____

_____

_____

Can you share with me something from our culture you wish for me to carry forward?

_____

_____

_____

_____

_____

The history of our culture is the history of who we are. We can reawaken the roots under the soles of our feet through engagement with our elders. We just need to seek with open curiosity, embody traditional cultural practices, and embrace our stories every step of the way.

Convocar Reflection: In the End, We Always Remember

My ancestors roamed this land before borders and before colonialism almost extinguished a culture rich in history, brilliance, and strength. My story did not start with my parents' migration to America, nor did it end with colonialism. My story started centuries ago, in Mesoamerica where my kin grew corn and studied the stars. They were artisans and scholars. They constructed pyramids and built communities. Knowing I am part of that history gives me a sense of pride and fills me with inspiration. I have always belonged to this story, no matter how we were pressured to assimilate. It was the act of embracing the places and people from which I descend that gave me back the parts of myself I didn't even know were lost.

What connects us and our ancestors? Simple—it is blood, DNA, breath, bone, imprint, and curiosity. It is by being active participants in seeking and honoring their memory that we connect the roots of our feet with the bodies, strengths, talents, and wisdom of our ancestors. We can form strong connections by listening, even if we are connecting with someone who has passed away. Our culture can come alive again when we study historical books tied to our ancestors and reclaim our cultural traditions, foods, or music. We cannot build a relationship to self if we do not build a relationship to our ancestors. They are a reflection of who we are, and when we engage in honoring them, we engage in honoring ourselves. When we foster a connection with our roots, we see all the ways we are like our ancestors. We may discover common goals and traits, and maybe even get a glimpse of what made them laugh. Remember, all connections begin with the spark of curiosity.

I embrace all that I was and all that I am becoming. I welcome all that I am yet to be. I am vibrant and vibrating with the hum of becoming.

A gentle word of warning, dear friend, reconnecting to our cultural roots and the history of our families can bring up a lot of emotions. You may learn difficult truths. It is not easy when we discover the painful stories of our ancestors. In those instances, it's okay to go slow and to give yourself time and space to process what you're feeling. Our ancestors may not have been perfect. Some could have troubled pasts. But we hold the potential for redemption with our existence, if we live true to our imprint.

As we share stories, celebrate our history, and honor our cultural traditions, may we feel the pulse of our ancestors' hearts through our chest. May we remember that we are alive because of those who came before us. We summon that which has always existed. We remember that regardless of the intentional erasure and cruelty of colonialism, we summon a rich history. What was lost is never forgotten. In the end, we always remember.

Shortened Incantation

I embrace all that I was and all I am becoming. I welcome all that I am yet to be. I am vibrant and vibrating with the hum of becoming.

Convocar Ritual

PLANTING SEEDS WITH OUR ANCESTORS

In this ritual, I invite you to plant a flower, herb, or plant in honor of your ancestors. Connecting to our Madre Tierra is a powerful way to connect to our ancestors, as our ancestors were people of the earth—living by her cycles and eating from her abundance.

When we plant a flower, herb, or seed to honor our ancestors, we nurture a relationship with them every day through tending to these plants. As we water the soil, we are watering the bond with our ancestor(s), so it may continue to grow and blossom.

You may plant any seed you wish. Or, you may choose to plant a particular herb or flower to which your ancestor(s) had a deep connection. If you do not know, I invite you to close your eyes and be guided intuitively in picking a flower, herb, or seed that you feel they would love. Here are the steps to this ritual:

- Choose your plant, flower, herb, or seed and designate a space for planting.
- On a sheet of compostable or biodegradable paper, handwrite a letter to the ancestor(s) you are honoring. The letter must indicate why you are planting this particular plant, flower, or seed. Write the ways you will be tending to it, and what you wish the outcome to be for the plant. Fold the paper into a small square.
- Make a small hole in the soil for your ancestor plant. Insert your letter into the hole and intentionally envision your ancestor receiving the letter. Be sure to leave extra space for your plant.
- Sprinkle some soil on top of the letter and then add your plant. Fill in the rest of the hole with soil.
- Water, tend, talk, pray, dance, and love on this plant, flower, or seed in honor of your ancestor(s). Speak to it as if it is your ancestor(s) in flesh before you. Commit to the tending of the plant. As it grows, you will also see the bond between you and your ancestor(s) grow.

Y *así es* (and so it is).

encarnar

Offering Eight

Encarnar
(Embody)

Incantation

When I turn to embodiment, I am turning to the magician in me—remembering that through the body, all spells, rituals, and incantations become manifested. It is in the body that all languages are transmuted into powerful incantations. I remember that I have the power to embody all magic within and around me, honoring the imprint of who I am.

Shortened Incantation

It is through the alchemy of embodiment that I awaken the magic around me and rooted within me. I embody the ancient powers of all creation.

Encarnar,
Una Fabúla

On a warm summer evening, an elder sat around the fire with his children, the embers illuminating his amber eyes. "Long ago," he began, "before our lands were split into barricaded declarations of ownership by conquistadores, ancient giants roamed Earth. They were nomads, traveling freely with their families from coast to coast in search of the next peaceful place to rest. They were not perceived as immigrants nor vagabonds, because the land was for everyone."

The children leaned forward, the orange glow of the fire lighting up their faces as they listened attentively without blinking.

The elder continued: "No one fought over land back then. Earth was regarded as sacred, and declaring ownership over it was a great sin. This land is for everyone and belongs to no one." The elder gestured with his hands, casting shadows across the faces of his children as he spoke. "The giants were mighty and sturdy, strong and resilient. Their dream was to find a place to call home, to live in harmony with the land, and raise their families in peace. Some realized their dream and found magnificent lands. They lived there happily for centuries, raising families and growing old. Eventually the giants passed away and became one with the earth. Their bones turned to stone and lush greenery grew over their bodies. This is how mountains came to be. Many, many years later, children, we can look to the mountains to be reminded of the strength of the giants. We can embody their resounding power and resilience as we walk upon their ancient bodies."

The elder closed his eyes, sitting in silence for a moment as the children gazed at the mountains on the horizon. "Our mountains are sacred," the elder continued. "They are our ancestral families, reminding us from afar that we come from mighty forces and we hold breathtaking beauty within us. Always look to the mountains when you need strength."

I created this story with the intention of passing it on to the next generation of my lineage. The mountains, or sleeping giants, that surround me have always filled me with vitality and hope. They remind me of *mi familia*'s journey of migration, the journey that brought me where I am today. They remind me of the resilience I carry and the strength of my once-undocumented parents. When I find myself questioning my capabilities, I look to the mountains and embody their power, beauty, and wisdom. I allow myself to be mesmerized by their height, their curves, and their undeniable presence. When I stare into the mountains, I remember who I am and why I do the work I do. The mountains carry my incantations. It is with the ancient wisdom of those ancestral sleeping giants that I gift these sacred prayers and practices to you. I invite you, dear friend, to embody the powerful magic in every word. May you always be reminded of your strength.

In 2016, I was diagnosed with type two diabetes—a chronic condition that affects the way the body processes sugar and can cause severe health complications. This came as no surprise to me. Growing up, I watched my *abuelas*, *tias* and *amá* struggle with diabetes. They would take medication or inject insulin to treat the illness, so it became a familiar part of our daily routine. I knew it was a possibility that I would also contract this illness due to genetics, but I never realized how it would impact my life. When my family members were diagnosed, they would alter what they eat, take their medication, and call it a day. When I first got diagnosed, I did the same, not giving it much attention, as it seemed normal in my family. I thought I'd be fine.

Months after my diagnosis, I came to understand how diabetes would impact my life, physically, emotionally, and spiritually. There was an internal shift, knowing I'd have to depend on this little white pill to maintain my blood sugar levels. Without it, I'd experience fatigue, headaches, shakiness, and other troubling symptoms. My body was no longer working on its own natural cycle, it needed external support. I didn't like that idea at all, so I became distant from my own body. I resented and rejected it. I felt like my body was faulty and damaged.

If I wanted to heal my relationship with my body, I needed to approach my health through a sympathetic lens. I started to do more research and I learned how connected the history of our health is to the history of colonialism. The essay "History as a Determinant of Health" by Dr. Sandro Galea at Boston University states in part: "The social, economic, and environmental conditions that shape the health of populations are not just the products of contemporary circumstance; they are part of an historical continuum. The effect that historical factors like war, economics, intellectual movements, and mass migration can have on the long-term health of populations argues for a consideration of the past itself as a determinant of health. . . ."[5] In other words, the illnesses many of us experience in today's society may be due to systemic issues, not just from unfortunate genetics. Everyone's health origins are different so of course this does not apply to all.

Present day colonialism, also known as neocolonialism, is an ongoing oppressive operation that harms Indigenous communities on a global scale in the modern day. Many Indigenous communities still don't have access to clean water, food, and basic health care. They've been denied access to their lands, which impacts their access to nutritious foods via agriculture, fishing, or hunting.

Neocolonialism today is also seen in the intentional disparities between the accessibility of grocery stores in low-income, rural, and ethnic minority neighborhoods versus middle- and higher-income neighborhoods. According to the Food Research & Action Center:

Disparities in food insecurity are a result of the structural racism originating with colonization and continuing to the present. Historical traumas have impacted traditional foodways, or the connection between culture, community, and the production and consumption of food. These traumas include the loss of food sovereignty from the forced relocation of AIAN (American Indian and Alaska Native) people from ancestral lands, forced cultural assimilation policies, disrupted land management and fractionation, Tribal termination and land privatization, and the substitution of Native culturally appropriate foods with commodity foods. Barriers to obtaining Native traditional food include permits limiting access to hunting, discriminatory farm-lending practices, fishing or farming, and degradation of the environment, while barriers to buying healthy food include the lack of transportation and the higher cost of food in Tribal areas.

Access to preparing healthy food is limited in those areas lacking electricity or running water.[6]

When people are unable to access healthy foods and have no option but to eat processed foods that are high fat, high sugar, and high salt, health problems manifest in the community. The doctor told me I needed to change my lifestyle so I could manage my health. I grew up on food stamps in a low-income neighborhood. My "lifestyle" wasn't my choice, it was the only option accessible to my parents. And my lifestyle leading up to my diagnosis was most certainly a reflection of that same upbringing. Processed foods were the only foods accessible to me due to my financial struggles, which can also be tied to colonization. Our lifestyle choices can directly impact our health and even bring us to our deathbed. However, for many of us, this lifestyle was not a choice. Our society needs to do better than just telling people to make healthier lifestyle choices. We need to make healthy choices available by removing the obstacles set up by oppressive systems in marginalized communities.

I decided to build decolonized practices that would help me heal my relationship to my physical body. Knowing our history is a vital part of understanding our bodies and what ails them through a compassionate and understanding lens, but that's only part of the treatment. We must call attention to the disconnection that happens within the body when disease is present. To reconnect ourselves, from imprint to flesh, we must become embodied creatures. We must decide we will no longer live by the ways of our colonizing oppressors. Instead, we must live by the ways of our ancestors, honoring their sacred rituals and practices.

What heals us medically is not always what heals us spiritually. We are not only body, organs, bones, blood, intestines, heart, brain, and muscle, we are also spirit—we are also imprint. Embodiment is the wellness of our imprint as a whole. Decolonizing our mind, body, and spirit, means no longer viewing ourselves in sections isolated by borders, but acknowledging that the physical, emotional, and spiritual are all weaved into one. While it's true that I need my medication, I no longer depend on it as my sole source of wellness. I believe this can be true for all of us. Our health solutions are not just found in a sterile medical office. They can be also found in nature, in the body, in reconnection, in our imprint.

Embodiment liberates us from everyone and everything that has made us believe we are inferior and in lack. Through embodiment, we become the creators of our own destiny—of our own wellness. It is in embodiment that we give ourselves access to what has been stolen. I can only imagine now how different the lives of my *abuelas, tias,* and *amá* might have been if they hadn't been denied access to a healthier lifestyle. I wonder if maybe their neutral reactions toward their diagnoses weren't as careless or uninformed as I thought. Maybe they knew of embodiment intuitively and found accessible ways to heal themselves. By growing their own foods when they could, by the *remedios* (remedies) that filled up their kitchen cabinets, through the *limpia* (cleansing) rituals of the body and spirit performed late into the night, by becoming an entire force of persistence, they demonstrated embodiment.

In the following pages, I will guide you through more in-depth practices of embodiment, and how you can use them in your journey to reconnect with your body. Allow yourself to be guided, not just by reading the words, but inviting these exercises, practices, and rituals into your bone, blood, and spirit.

The Power of Embodiment

Embodiment is defined as the "tangible or visible form of an idea, quality, or feeling." I like to define embodiment as bringing something to life by using the body as the medium. Whether that be a phrase, a single word, a song, an image, a spell, or even an object, we must be willing to completely open ourselves to receiving. To understand embodiment is to understand that everything holds an energy that can be tapped and experienced.

There is a difference between being present in your body and only living in your body. When we experience trauma, medical illnesses, environmental racism, lack of food supply, poverty, or abuse, we can become disconnected from our bodies. We disassociate because being present and fully experiencing certain emotions all at once can be too painful. To survive, we disconnect.

After the diagnosis of my chronic illness, I disassociated from my body and internalized the pain and resentment I felt. I hated the fact that I suddenly had to rely on medication to stay stable. It wasn't until I landed in the hospital, close to a diabetic coma, that I realized how badly I needed to reconnect with my body so I could be receptive to its messages. I never allowed my body the space to process my diagnosis. Instead of learning to live with diabetes, I did my best to ignore it. I knew I needed to create a new relationship with food and make lifestyle changes to honor my sacred body. It was a different way of existing, different from the way my relatives had approached their health, but I knew it was necessary for my health.

I started having conversations with my body, not just when I was sick, but every day. My practice began with sitting still and attuning to all my senses, allowing my body to communicate with me, allowing each emotion to be felt. This reconnection allowed me to listen and understand what my body was telling me about what it needed to heal and be healthy. Many times, we are given a "quick fix," like a pill or surgery. Sometimes those quick fixes disconnect us further from our own bodies. Embodiment allows us to bring the messages of our bodies into the discussion with medical professionals. I am not advising anyone to disregard medical advice. However, I am encouraging you to become an advocate for your body through a respectful communication that acknowledges its needs.

We are creatures driven by the senses. It is through the senses that we understand our surroundings and ourselves. When we open ourselves to our senses, we are also opening ourselves to the energy of the magic around us, from the strength of the mountains to the serenity of a lake. Every one of our senses can serve as a gateway to our embodiment journey. With our senses awakened, we can access the forces in our environment to empower us as we face all the beauty and challenges in our lives.

Embodiment Exercise: Awakening Your Strength

In this exercise, I will guide you through an embodiment journey that will help you awaken your strength through your senses. If strength is not something you wish to awaken in this moment, feel free to swap "strength" in this exercise with whatever feeling or emotion you wish to awaken.

- I invite you to close your eyes and take three deep breaths.
- Cultivate an image of what strength (or your chosen trait) means to you. Is it a sleeping giant like the ones in my fable at the beginning of this chapter? Is it a family member? It is the tall trees or buildings in the city where you live? Is it your partner or friend?
- Once you have that image, I want you to take that image and transmute it into a feeling of strength. You can do this by using your senses to taste, smell, feel, and hear what strength means to you. Let your senses be a gateway into what strength symbolizes.
- Allow yourself to fully embody what your senses are communicating, pulling their messages into your entire body. Feel it in your bones, taste it in your mouth, pay close attention to what you are hearing. Close or open your eyes and visualize the spirit of strength surrounding you.
- Now envision the image building to a feeling of empowerment. Allow it to straighten your back, lift your chin, balance your hip bones, steady your shoulders.
- Allow the image to slowly turn into a liquid substance, trickling down into your throat, then your chest, into your arms, down through your belly and hip bones, flowing down to your knees and feet. Allow strength to fill you up and flow through your body.
- Come back to this embodiment exercise as often as you would like, and feel free to interchange the traits you wish to embody.

Embodiment is a crucial part of our liberation. The more we disconnect from our truth—our imprint—the more easily we can be manipulated into betraying ourselves. Oppressive forces seek to turn our bodies into war zones, for example, through the banishment of reproductive healthcare for women, laws against LGBTQIA2S+ folks, and hateful immigration laws. But it is through embodiment that we can ignite our rebellion against these systems. We rebel by fully embracing and living in the truth of our bodies and our history. We rebel by honoring every bone, every stream of blood, every muscle, organ, and skin cell. We connect even deeper with ourselves through embodiment, because embodiment is freedom.

Practice: Embodiment Art

Embodiment can be attained through dancing, writing, performing, singing, cooking, or any other activity that connects you to the magic around you. Initially, writing poetry infused my imprint with words of healing and self-discovery. Later, it was drawing and illustrating that allowed me to embody the energy of my art. There are many ways to work with the magic of embodiment. If you are like me, an artist who has struggled with disconnection from the body, a sketching or a drawing practice is a helpful tool in becoming embodied. The following is a drawing practice that can guide you in becoming embodied. You do not need to be an artist to do this practice. Remember that your drawings don't have to be perfect. What matters is the intention behind what you're drawing. I have intentionally left the image on the next page incomplete to give you room to fill it in with the components you wish to embody.

- Fill in the body with the facial expression you wish to embody (maybe this is a peaceful expression, a resilient expression, etc.).

- Add components to the clothing that represent what you wish to embody. You may choose to add flowers to embody softness, flames for fierceness, wings to embody liberation, or a peaceful, colored aura to embody peace.
- Draw elements to the image to express a visual representation of the energy you wish to embody.

everything about me is
sacred ceremony

One of the first drawings I ever created after my diagnosis was of a nude woman sitting in a butterfly position. There were dainty pink and purple flowers sprouting behind her. She had one hand on her heart and the other on her womb. I wrote the following words below the illustration: *"Everything about me is sacred ceremony."* I drew this because I was searching for a deep understanding of my body.

Drawing nude bodies helped me heal the way I perceived my body. I opened my mind so I could see how beautiful soft bellies can be, how curves and rolls are like the mountains, and how stretch marks tell a story of all the beautiful experiences of our lives. When I drew the illustration of the naked woman, I embodied the feeling of deep reverence for my body. The sprouting flowers behind her signified our potential for growth, when we allow ourselves to evolve. The hand to her heart reminded me to trust myself even if I don't know the next step. The other hand to the belly portrayed the idea that I am more than just a source of procreation. And the words, *Everything about me is sacred ceremony,* were a declaration that I don't need to change anything about myself. I'm already sacred and everything I need to be.

Whether I knew it in that moment or not, each line, each component was formulated intentionally to help me embody the message of deep respect and admiration for my body. Journaling and drawing have helped me heal and understand myself. I look at all of the illustrations I've drawn as portals to magical realms of healing and peace. If I sought strength, I drew images of empowerment, motivation, and resilience. If I sought softness, I drew delicate images, such as butterflies and flowers. Drawing and writing are essential parts of my embodiment.

Encarnar Journal Prompts

Embodiment isn't always about healing, it contains many benefits and can be practiced through many mediums. We can embody patience, beauty, ease, or wisdom, as well as healing. Embodiment can be used if we need to de-stress our bodies. For instance, we can activate our embodiment to de-stress and bring us back to a state of ease by shaking and moving the body while envisioning our worries and stressors sliding off our bodies. As we shake and move, we can invite ease and flow to replace our worries and stressors.

To create an embodiment practice that is catered to your unique needs, it's helpful to start with the following steps and journaling prompts:

Sit comfortably, get still, and check in with your body. Ask yourself: If my ailments in need of healing could express themselves, what part of my body would they use?

As you ask yourself the previous question, pay attention to sensations in your body. Which parts are awakening to your question? Maybe your hand tingles with an urge to move? Are your hips feeling activated, as if they want to sway? Is your belly asking you to feed it? Is your throat opening to say something? Document your experience below.

_____

_____

_____

_____

_____

As these areas of your body communicate with you, what are they sharing? How do they wish to be healed? What do they need to be back in balance and harmony?

_____

_____

_____

_____

_____

Pay attention to each of these areas. Your body will tell you where embodiment is needed. Write any final observations here.

_____

_____

_____

_____

_____

When doing the practices of embodiment, you may also look to your environment for inspiration. Maybe the strength of the mountains, the cool flow of a stream, or the soft floating clouds can inspire you. If you feel called to do so, you may create stories about the inspiring things in your environment that you wish to embody, like I did with my story about the giants that became mountains at the beginning of this offering. My art and stories help me embody the power and beauty in nature. Feel free to create a practice that resonates with you. If you are not inclined to create art or stories, you may choose to meditate in nature, take a mindful walk, dance, lie on the grass and look at the clouds, or observe the beauty around you. Remember, anything can be embodied. The meaning comes from you. You may choose to keep it private or share it with others. Embodiment is a personal and unique journey.

Final Reflection: Incantations Embodied

I invite you to make this formula part of your daily life:

Incantation (spirit/understanding) + Embodiment (the body/expression) = Living in harmony in our external and internal worlds.

Our imprint is nourished by incantations, rituals, exercises, and practices that reconnect us to our most liberated, wise, and compassionate selves. Incantations and embodiment are tied together in a delicate balance. We need both to live in our truth and in harmony with our internal and external worlds.

It is my wish for you to allow the essence of this book to flow through you, to embody every word, through every practice, exercise, and ritual. May the words in these pages encourage you to live in the honesty of who you are and not in the shadow of your pains, struggles, or oppression. Living as incantations embodied means we thrive regardless of any obstacle in our path. Incantations embodied means we choose joy, remembrance, healing, perspective, nature, and we honor our lineages. With these practices we declare that we are worthy of waking up every day knowing what it means to live in the essence of our imprint, our highest, most worthy, most magnificent selves. May you live in this honor.

Shortened Incantation

It is through the alchemy of embodiment that I awaken the magic around me and rooted within me. I embody the ancient powers of all creation.

Encarnar Ritual

DRAWING YOUR EMBODIMENT

Art is a practice that can help us understand and express how we are feeling. It can also be nice to have something physical to come back to and look at when we need a reminder of our commitment to embodiment. Feel free to fill in the image on the next page with the following suggestions for embodiment:

It is through the alchemy of embodiment that I awaken the magic around me and rooted within me. I embody the powers of all creation.

- Color each body part with a color that you wish to embody. Colors hold and represent certain energies. Here is a quick guide to what some colors represent:

  White: safety and presence

  Black: protection and power

  Red: strength and love

  Pink: sweetness and compassion

  Orange: confidence and bravery

  Yellow: happiness and creativity

  Green: healing and nourishment

  Blue: peace and faith

  Purple: spirituality and ambition

  Brown: dependability and trustworthiness

- Draw on each body part what you wish to embody. For example, you can draw flowers growing from the chest to symbolize outgrowing things that no longer fit and blooming into a new, more beautiful version of you.
- Write a poem with words you wish to embody on a part of the body you want to affect. You may also write an embodiment poem on the entire body, if you wish it to affect your whole being.
- Use cutouts from magazines, old books, collected poems or downloaded images and paste them onto the body. Using imagery is a powerful way to connect to that image and embody what you are trying to express.
- Or, you can simply fill a body part with the color of the energy you wish to achieve.

Come back to this image as often as you like. At the completion of this ritual, speak out loud, hum under your breath, or feel this phrase in your bones:

Y así es (and so it is).
This ritual is complete.

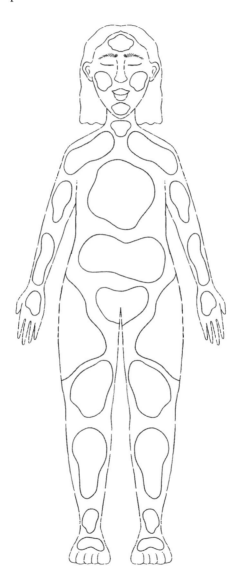

This Isn't Goodbye . . .

Dearest friend,

This isn't the end of your *viaje* (journey). It is only the beginning of a magnificent adventure full of triumph, growth, grief, and living in your truth. Your path is uniquely perfect for you because, as we've learned in this book, we define our own acceptance. It is not determined by a colonized system of oppression. You now get to choose how to live on your own terms. May you walk boldly, undefined and driven only by the imprint of your spirit. I wish for you to remember this:

You are everything sacred made into flesh,
a prayer when speaking,
a meditation when sitting,
a spell when singing,
a temple when loving,
and an entire force
when intention and devotion fill your heart.

I am so proud of you for taking the leap to find yourself amid the barriers that you have encountered. You are resilient and capable of unbinding yourself from the generational trauma that has taunted your lineage. You deserve to know peace. You deserve to know what loving yourself free from the bondage of shame feels like. I am rooting for you every step of the way, and I hold you in my prayers. As you close this book today, know that you may come back to it as often as needed. When you are faced with worries, with feeling a bit lost or discouraged, know that this safe haven is here to remind you why you are on this path. It is okay to need a reminder occasionally. If you find yourself feeling disoriented or unsure, sing or recite this prayer:

> I will light a candle,
> and chant until I become a prayer.
> I am the child of wolf and eagle,
> resilient by nature,
> a beaming love by right.
> A force in the distance,
> a reflection of persistence.
> I am the rain that insists on pouring,
> the river that continues to flow.
> I am infused with all that exists,
> And all that is yet to become.

As you walk the red road,[7] remember that you are not alone. Not only am I with you, walking in prayer, but there are also countless other kin who are walking alongside you as well. There are others who are on a similar journey as yours. Your ancestors are with you, rooting for you at every turn. Madre Tierra, who has crafted you from her arms, embraces you. The elements, which you carry within you, grant you access to all of their powers. The universe pours from your hands. We are all with you. Close your eyes and feel the prayers from all of us radiating through the center of your chest. Feel the warmth that is building and the vibration that is rising—that is us, here with you.

A final ritual that I invite you to do with this book is this:

Take this book and venture outside, whether it is a physical copy of this book, a digital copy, or the audio version playing from your device. Place the book on the ground and put your hand on top of it. I invite you to make the following vow and become, here in this moment, the altar that will carry you forth. Recite the following incantation to complete the spell of embodiment:

Today I vow
to become the altar of my own choosing.
I will adorn myself with fresh flowers,
Bury my feet in soil,
And remember my bones are the portals to the wisdom I carry.
Today I vow
to welcome the sacred directions of the east, west, south, and north.
I will let my passion be the candles that light my way,
my blood will be the ancestral force that guides me,
my breath, the sacred prayers that protect me.
Today I vow
to let the sacred medicine of Madre Tierra embrace me.
I will give in to my magic and let it surround me.
I will honor it by always being true to who I am
and never alter parts of me simply because they are different.
Today and every day
I am glorious.
I am the ritual that never fades,
the incantation that always sings,
the embodiment that always paves the way.
Today I vow
to choose me.
Y *así es.*
And so it is.

Tlazohcamati,

Kimberly Rodriguez

Acknowledgments

I would like to thank my ancestors whose sacred medicine flows through me as I actively walk the path of reclamation and remembrance. It is through their prayers and rituals that I am here today, living in my truth through their truth.

To my parents, I wrote you a poem long ago that has collected dust in my old journal and deserves to live among these pages:

Even with the moon at its peak
and the tallest mountain demanding to be seen,
You will always be the scenery worth painting.
You will always be the story worth telling.
You will always be the light worth gazing.
You will always be the struggle worth sharing.

Thank you, Amá y Apá, for showing me what courage and resilience can look like. Thank you for your dedication to gifting your children with opportunities that neither of you had access to when you were young. This book is a token of your efforts. I love you, my *viejitos*.

To my siblings, Daniela, Alejandra, and Erik, we traveled through the same womb, and we have traveled through the same journey of healing and discovery. It is safe to say we will continue to travel together, laughing, crying, and hugging one another along the way. Thank you for sharing my joy in the publication of this book. Love you all!

To my husband, whose kindness, patience and love take my breath away. I thought people like you were only in fairy tales, but fairy tales are put to shame with your presence. You make loving you so easy. Thank you for supporting and encouraging me as I focused on crafting this book. When my nervous system was triggered, thank you for holding me late into the nights, whispering and soothing me to sleep, reminding me that I deserve to be here, writing this book. You are a beautiful human, *amor, te amo*!

To my editor, Jamie Lou, thank you for helping me visualize and craft *Incantations Embodied* to become bigger than I had initially intended. Your vision for the medicine I wished to share has made this book a wondrous experience for our beloved readers. Thank you for the many pep talks and sharing the excitement with me as I wrote my story among these pages. You are a genius!

And finally, to my publisher, Spirit Bound Press—wow! What an honor to be among your first authors. Thank you for believing in my story and the medicine I wished to share. Thank you for amplifying my voice and allowing me to make my ancestors even more proud by giving my story a home in your press. You are creating changes not only in publishing but within many communities. So proud to be published by you.

Tlazohcamati.

Appendix
Image Descriptions

CONJURO/INTRODUCTION

The image is presented inside a long square with detailed edges made up of long swirly vines and flower heads on all four edges of the long square. At the bottom center of the long square the word *conjuro* is displayed in bold text. The image inside of the long square is of a female presenting person with two long braids flowing in the wind. They are barefoot and wearing a floral printed dress with a striped apron tied at the waist. They have their eyes closed and are holding a flute to their mouth. Flowing out of the flute are thin lines made up of magical specs of stars and among the magical specs of stars are two birds flying intertwined as if they are flowing and dancing with the song of the flute. The female presenting person is standing on top of a large flower with its petals open and relaxing downward. Surrounding the female presenting person are bushy flowers, long vines, and floral stems all sprouting around. At the top middle left side of the image lays a crescent moon with a relaxed face.

DISIPANDO/PART ONE

The image is presented inside a long square with detailed edges made up of long swirly vines and flower heads on all four edges of the long square. At the bottom center of the long square the word *disipando* is displayed in bold text.

The image inside of the long square is of four individuals in an outdoor setting. The setting displays a large bushy tree on the left side of the image and in the far background lays tall mountains with a river streaming down from the top to the bottom. Displayed on the ground are streaks of long grass. There are three individuals standing up and one individual sitting down in front of the three standing individuals in a meditation position. All four individuals are holding a lit candle up to their chest and they all have their eyes closed. The individual sitting down in meditation position is a female presenting person. They have their hair braided and pinned in a circle on their head forming a crown. They are wearing a floral-patterned vest and a short sleeve dress. The individual standing up to the left is a male presenting person. They have short hair that reaches to their chin. They are wearing a short sleeve top with patterned circles along the sleeve hemline and circled tassels coming from the bottom of the top hemline. They are wearing pants with circle tassels coming from the bottom of the hemline. The individual standing up in the center is a female presenting elder with their hair pinned up in a bun. They are wearing a short sleeve dress with a floral pattern on the sleeve hemline, and they are wearing a striped sleeveless apron dress. The individual standing up to the right is a female presenting person with two braids hanging down past their shoulders. They are wearing a short sleeve dress that drapes down to their ankles. The dress has a floral pattern along the center of the dress.

·

DESENREDAR/OFFERING ONE

The image is presented inside a long square with detailed edges made up of long swirly vines and flower heads on all four edges of the long square. At the bottom center of the long square the word *desenredar* is displayed in bold text. The image inside of the long square is of a lagoon. Surrounding the lagoon are many flowers and vines sprouting from every direction. There is a dragonfly flying in the left side of the image. In the center of the lagoon there is a female presenting head floating. The rest of the body is submerged inside the water and only the head is sprouting above the surface and laying on its side. The female presenting head has their eyes closed and half of their face is underwater. They have long black hair that is floating and laid out in various directions among the water surface.

✺

OFFERING ONE—ENDING

The image is presented inside a long square with detailed edges made up of long swirly vines and flower heads on all four edges of the long square. At the bottom center of the long square the phrase "I expand beyond measure, for I do not need to shrink myself to feel loved or accepted. I see myself for who I am and who I wish to be, and I find beauty in that" is displayed in bold text. The image inside of the long square is of a lagoon with many flowers and vines sprouting from every direction. In the center of the lagoon floating on a water leaf sits a female presenting person. They have their eyes closed and their face expresses a relaxed emotion. They have long black hair and are nude. They have their hands extended outward besides their hips and their long black hair drapes over their fingers and down to the water. Various strands of their hair are floating on the water. There is a dragonfly standing on the female presenting persons' leg.

✺

RECLAMAR/OFFERING TWO

The image is presented inside a long square with detailed edges made up of long swirly vines and flower heads on all four edges of the long square. At the bottom center of the long square the word *reclamar* is displayed in bold text. The image inside of the long square is presented in an outdoor setting. There are two female presenting people. The person to the left of the image is kneeling and planting on the ground an outgrown plant. Surrounding the person on the left are various growing plants. There is a small shovel to the left of them and an empty basket to the right of them. This female presenting person is wearing a long sleeve top and long pants. They have on a sleeveless apron. The top part of the apron has a floral pattern, and the bottom part of the apron has a striped pattern. They have short curly hair that extends out as an aura surrounding their head. They are wearing a black band on their head. The person on the right side is weaving a piece of fabric on an ancestral weaving tool made up of wood. They are sitting down in a meditation position holding the weaving tool in front of them. The weaving tool has two pieces of wood standing up a few inches apart from each other and tied in a flat surface in front of them are various other pieces of wood in order to form a flat surface. On the weaving tool lays an already made-up piece of weaved fabric. The person has long hair and in front of their face drapes three small braids. They are wearing a long sleeve dress and a poncho is draped over them that has a squared pattern. They are sitting on top of a floral-patterned blanket. Behind the two female presenting people to the right is a strong rooted tree with bushy archways going in many directions. The tree has a face of an elder and is looking at the two female presenting people in front of them with happiness. The tree is blowing out magical dust from their lips and sending prayers of strength and love to the two female presenting people in front of them. Beyond the tree are tall mountains.

OFFERING TWO—ENDING

The image is presented inside a long square with detailed edges made up of long swirly vines and flower heads on all four edges of the long square. At the bottom center of the long square the phrase "I am the altar at which I pray. I am the Ancestor in becoming. I am the magic and all the chaos. I am purpose and destiny, voyage and arrival, reclamation and truth. I trust in myself and step into my power" is displayed in bold text. The image inside of the long square is of two female presenting people in an outdoor setting. The person on the middle left is wearing a long sleeve top and long pants. They have on a sleeveless apron. The top part of the apron has a floral pattern, and the bottom part of the apron has a striped pattern. They have short curly hair that extends out as an aura surrounding their head. They are wearing a black band on their head. They are holding a corn cob and filling up their basket that already has many pieces of corn inside. Behind them is a tall cornfield with many of the plants having corn exposed. The female presenting person on the right has long hair and in front of their face drapes three small braids. They are wearing a long sleeve dress and a poncho is draped over them that has a squared pattern. They are holding a piece of fabric that they just weaved with their ancestral weaving tool. In front of them lays their ancestral weaving tool on top of a floral blanket on the ground. The weaving tool has two pieces of wood standing up a few inches apart from each other and tied in a flat surface in front of them are various other pieces of wood in order to form a flat surface. Behind the two female presenting people are tall mountains and a tree to the right with bushy leaves extending in many directions. The tree has an elder face to it with swirly prints imprinted on their cheeks and forehead. They have a happy relaxed facial expression.

·

CULTIVAR/PART TWO

The image is presented inside a long square with detailed edges made up of long swirly vines and flower heads on all four edges of the long square. At the bottom center of the long square the word *cultivar* is displayed in bold text. The image is of a female presenting person who is nude. They have long black hair that drapes down to the floor. Their hair has shimmering sparkles all over it. They have their hands resting beside their side with their palms facing out. A sun outline is embedded on their right hand and a crescent moon is embedded on their left hand. The female presenting body has their eyes closed and they have an additional eye on the center of their forehead that is open and looking straight ahead. There is a spiral embedded on the center of their chest, a lit candle on the center of their stomach, and a flower petal on the center of their abdomen. They have sprouted leaves, mushrooms, and vines from the top of their feet. The vines are spiraling up to their side and all the way to the top, reaching far higher than them. There are tiny leaves and apples that are sprouting from these vines.

LIBERAR/OFFERING THREE

The image is presented inside a long square with detailed edges made up of long swirly vines and flower heads on all four edges of the long square. At the bottom center of the long square the word *liberar* is displayed in bold text. The image is of an outdoor setting. There are big leaves with vines sprouting from the bottom corners of the image and an extending tree branch propping from the right top side. From the tree branch, hangs a bird cage with a hummingbird caged in. Next to the cage is a gender nonconforming person. They have short black hair that is slicked back and are wearing a cowboy hat. They have on a long sleeve shirt with a dotted pattern going from the top of the shoulders down to the mid-bottom center of the top. They are wearing a scarf that cinches in the center with a floral brooch. They have on long pants with a circular pattern along the bottom hemline. Their facial expression is that of grief and pain. They are carrying a key on their right hand and a bowl of water on their left hand.

OFFERING THREE—ENDING

The image is presented inside a long square with detailed edges made up of long swirly vines and flower heads on all four edges of the long square. At the bottom center of the long square the phrase "I do not let others make me feel ashamed of who I am or who I wish to be. I see value in being me and freely pursue all things that bring me joy" is displayed in bold text. The image is of an outdoor setting. There are big leaves with vines sprouting from the bottom corners of the image and an extending tree branch propping from the right top side. There is a bird cage that has fallen to the floor and the door is open. On the left side, flies a hummingbird that has just been freed from the cage. On the right side is a gender nonconforming person. They have short black hair that is slicked back and are wearing a cowboy hat. They have on a long sleeve shirt with a dotted pattern going from the top of the shoulders down to the mid-bottom center of the top. They are wearing a scarf that cinches in the center with a floral brooch. They have on long pants with a circular pattern along the bottom hemline. They have on happy and relieved facial expression. They have on their left hand a knife and on their right hand, a piece of the rope that had at one point tied the bird cage to the tree branch.

INVOCAR/OFFERING FOUR

The image is presented inside a long square with detailed edges made up of long swirly vines and flower heads on all four edges of the long square. At the bottom center of the long square the word *invocar* is displayed in bold text. The image is of an apothecary room. In the center of the room is a round table with vine detailing along the tables' sides. On the table are candles, potion bottles, a tarot deck, floral vases, and an open spell book. Behind the round table is a female presenting person. They have short black hair and are wearing a long sleeve dress that drapes down to the floor. Their dress has a pointy collar that drapes down to their chest with a center tie. They are looking down at the spell book on the table and are pointing to a part of the book. They are holding a potion bottle labeled "magic" with their right hand. Behind the person are two bookshelves, one to the left and one to the right that are both similar in composition. They both hold spell bottles, books, plants in vases, and lit candles. Many of the spell bottles are labeled as "potion," "clarity," "love," "courage," "vision," "peace," "wisdom," "conjure," "protection," and "ancestor."

·

OFFERING FOUR—ENDING

The image is presented inside a long square with detailed edges made up of long swirly vines and flower heads on all four edges of the long square. At the bottom center of the long square the phrase "It's not a matter of who I'm not, but who I am that invokes who I will be" is displayed in bold text. The image is of an apothecary room. In the center, floating above all furniture in the room is a female presenting person. They are looking up toward the ceiling as if they have just invoked their magic. They have short black hair and are wearing a long sleeve dress. Their dress has a pointy collar that drapes down to their chest with a center tie. They are holding a five-edged star on their right hand and a magic wand on their left hand. Below the flying female presenting person is a round table with vine detailing along the table's sides. On the table are candles, potion bottles, a tarot deck, floral vases, and an open spell book. Behind the person are two bookshelves, one to the left and one to the right that are both similar in composition. They both hold spell bottles, books, plants in vases, and lit candles. Many of the spell bottles are labeled as "potion," "clarity," "love," "courage," "vision," "peace," "wisdom," "conjure," "protection," and "ancestor."

·

REVELACIÓN/PART THREE

The image is presented inside a long square with detailed edges made up of long swirly vines and flower heads on all four edges of the long square. At the bottom center of the long square the word *revelación* is displayed in bold text. The image is of a botanical setting. There are large flowers sprouted everywhere. In the center of the image, there is a female presenting elder sitting on one of the large flower heads as if it's a throne. The elder has a long braid that is swooped to the left side and drapes down to their hip. They have on a short sleeve patterned dress that drapes down to the floor. Their left breast is exposed. They are holding with their right hand a large sword. On their left hand lays a small black snake that is looped on their wrist. The elder has on a confident expression.

ENCANTAR/OFFERING FIVE

The image is presented inside a long square with detailed edges made up of long swirly vines and flower heads on all four edges of the long square. At the bottom center of the long square the word *encantar* is displayed in bold text. The image is of two male presenting individuals. They are facing each other with their palms facing outward and touching one another's palms. From their palms, there is a vibration rising, making an eye with a spiral. Both male presenting individuals are the same person. They both have short hair that swoops to one side. They are not wearing a shirt and have on long pants. They both have their eyes closed and have on a focused facial expression. To the side of them are flowers sprouting. Above them are three rabbits hopping over them going from left to right. Surrounding the entire image are particles of magical dust and stars.

OFFERING FIVE—ENDING

The image is presented inside a long square with detailed edges made up of long swirly vines and flower heads on all four edges of the long square. At the bottom center of the long square the phrase "I invite creativity to enchant me so I may always find myself and fully harness the power of my spirit" is displayed in bold text. The image is of a male presenting person. They are sitting down in a meditation position with their palms facing up and resting on their thighs. They are not wearing a shirt and have on long pants. They have their eyes closed and on the center of their forehead, there is an opened eye looking straight ahead. They have short hair that rests down to their cheeks. Behind them are flowers sprouting and on the right side there is a rabbit standing on one of the flowers holding a vase full of water and pouring it intentionally onto the male presenting persons' head. From the male presenting persons' head, there is a vine with petals sprouting.

CONJURAR/OFFERING SIX

The image is presented inside a long square with detailed edges made up of long swirly vines and flower heads on all four edges of the long square. At the bottom center of the long square the word *conjurar* is displayed in bold text. The image is of an outdoor setting. There are two female presenting individuals. The one of the left is kneeling down and has their hands raised to the sky. They have long hair that drapes down to their legs. They have on a sleeveless dress with a floral pattern that reaches above their knee. The person to the right is kneeling and holds a flame on their hands. They have short curly hair and have on a headwrap. They have on a short sleeve striped dress that reaches above their knees. In front of both individuals is a stack of wood logs. Behind both individuals are tall mountains with flowers sprouting all around. In the sky is a large shining crescent moon.

OFFERING SIX—ENDING

The image is presented inside a long square with detailed edges made up of long swirly vines and flower heads on all four edges of the long square. At the bottom center of the long square the phrase "I am the conjurer of strength, transmuting and shape-shifting everything that ails me and everything that pains me. I transmute my painful experiences to opportunities of growth and expansion" is displayed in bold text. The image is of an outdoor setting. There are two female presenting individuals dancing in front of a campfire. They are throwing their hands up and moving their legs. The individual to the left has long hair and is wearing a sleeveless floral-patterned dress that reaches above the knee. The individual to the right has on a stripped short sleeve dress that reaches above the knee. They are wearing a headwrap. They both have on a cheerful facial expression. Behind them are flowers sprouting everywhere and large mountains in the distance. There is a large shining crescent moon in the sky.

EXPRESIÓN/PART FOUR

The image is presented inside a long square with detailed edges made up of long swirly vines and flower heads on all four edges of the long square. At the bottom center of the long square the word *expresión* is displayed in bold text. The image is of a female presenting person. They are in a side view pose from the chest up looking up toward the sky. They have on a soft smile, and they have freckles along their cheeks made up of a small crescent moon and stars. They are wearing an off the shoulder top with a floral and striped print. From the center of their forehead there are specks of magical dust flowing out and wrapping themselves onto a full moon in the sky. Along the full moon in the sky, there are three flying crows. The person's hair is long and flowing above them in a circular motion. Intertwined in their hair are flowers sprouting out.

CONVOCAR/OFFERING SEVEN

The image is presented inside a long square with detailed edges made up of long swirly vines and flower heads on all four edges of the long square. At the bottom center of the long square the word *convocar* is displayed in bold text. The image is of a female presenting person in an outdoor setting. The female presenting person is standing in the center of the image and holding with their left arm a large flower with its stem as if it's a royalty rod. They have their right hand raised up to the sky with their palm facing to the right and next to it is a flying crow. In between their hand and crow are small specks of magical dust with a swirl in between. The person is wearing a long sleeve dress with small geometric details along the sides of the dress and along the sleeves of the dress. They are wearing a geometric patterned corset. They have curly hair that extends out behind them in an aura shape. They have on a floral crown on their head. They have a soft peaceful expression. From the persons' back, there are butterfly wings extending out. Behind the person, there are sprouting flowers growing in every direction.

OFFERING SEVEN—ENDING

The image is presented inside a long square with detailed edges made up of long swirly vines and flower heads on all four edges of the long square. At the bottom center of the long square the phrase "I embrace all that I was and all that I am becoming. I welcome all that I am yet to be. I am vibrant and vibrating with the hum of becoming" is displayed in bold text. The image is of a female presenting person and they are wearing a long sleeve dress with small geometric details along the sides of the dress and along the sleeves of the dress. They are wearing a geometric patterned corset. They have curly hair that extends out behind them in an aura shape. They have on a floral crown on their head with a crow's face as a mask. They are holding a tall rod with intricate detailing that has a crescent moon at the top of it. With their right hand, they are holding a butterfly. Behind the person, there is a scenery of the sky. There are clouds flouting in every direction and shining stars radiating.

ENCARNAR/OFFERING EIGHT

The image is presented inside a long square with detailed edges made up of long swirly vines and flower heads on all four edges of the long square. At the bottom center of the long square the word *encarnar* is displayed in bold text. The image is of three nude female presenting individuals who are all sitting down in large flower heads. Two of the individuals are sitting in the back and one is sitting in the center in front. The one in the front has two long braids draping over their shoulder and covering their breasts. They are holding an ancestral drum that has a small flower in the center of the drum. With their left hand, they are banging the drum. Their eyes are closed and have a swirl imprint on each cheek. The two individuals in the back look the same. They each have a hand on the person in front of them and with their other hand they are holding a floral wand that is burning. They both have long hair that drapes over their shoulder and covers their breasts. They have a swirling speck of magical particles wrapping around their head and extending out as if they are envisioning the prayers they are instilling in the person in front of them. Their eyes are closed, and they have swirl imprints on each of their cheeks.

OFFERING EIGHT—ENDING

The image is presented inside a long square with detailed edges made up of long swirly vines and flower heads on all four edges of the long square. At the bottom center of the long square the phrase "It is through the alchemy of embodiment that I awaken the magic around me and rooted within me. I embody the powers of all creation" is displayed in bold text. The image is of a female presenting person in an outdoor setting. They are wearing a long sleeve dress that has a striped pattern in the skirt area. They are holding a large human heart that has sprouted leaves coming out of it in all directions. The human heart has large roots sprouting down to the ground. The person has a peaceful expression with their eyes closed. From the center of their forehead, there are five sprouting rays that are each transforming into an item. Going from left to right, the first one is of a swirl, then the next one is of a five-edged star, following by a lit candle, then a rose, and finally a crescent moon. Behind the person are large bushes of flowers and foliage.

Notes

1. Clarissa Pinkola Estés, *Women Who Run with the Wolves: Myths and Stories of the Wild Woman Archetype* (New York: Ballantine Books, 2002).
2. Lawrence Robinson; Melinda Smith, and Jeanne Segal, "Laughter Is the Best Medicine," HelpGuide.org, February 28, 2023, https://www.help guide.org/articles/mental-health/laughter-is-the-best-medicine.htm.
3. Carolyn Newman, "The pandemic is increasing intimate partner violence. Here is how health care providers can help," UAB News, October 26, 2021, https://www.uab.edu/news/health/item/12390-the-pandemic-is-increasing -intimate-partner-violence-here-is-how-health-care-providers-can-help.
4. NCADV: National Coalition Against Domestic Violence, "Statistic" (n.d.), https://ncadv.org/STATISTICS.
5. Sandro Galea, "History as a Determinant of Health," Boston University School of Public Health, March 12, 2017, https://www.bu.edu/sph/news /articles/2017/history-as-a-determinant-of-health/.
6. A. M. Lacko and G. Henchy, *Hunger, Poverty, and Health Disparities during COVID-19 and the Federal Nutrition Programs' Role in an Equitable Recovery* (Washington, DC: Food Research & Action Center, September 2021), 16, https://frac.org/wp-content/uploads/COVIDResearchReport -2021.pdf.
7. The "Red Road" is a spiritual path, one where a person strengthens the physical, mental, and spiritual aspects of life in order to achieve harmony. It's comes from Native Americans.

About the Author

KIMBERLY RODRIGUEZ is a first-generation Xicana Indigena artist; her art reflects her journey toward reclaiming her indigenous roots and exploring different forms of self-expression. Kimberly's art visually represents her spiritual journey and commitment to celebrating diverse body types and experiences. Through her work, she aims to inspire others to embrace their unique identities and feel empowered in their skin. As an artist, Kimberly is deeply committed to creating work that is inclusive and accessible to all. She believes that art has the power to heal, connect, and inspire, and strives to use her platform to promote positivity and self-love. In addition to her art, Kimberly is also a writer and community activist. She is dedicated to using her talents and voice to create positive change and empower others to do the same. Overall, Kimberly's work is a testament to the transformative power of embracing one's truth and finding one's unique voice. Her art is a celebration of diversity, resilience, and the beauty that can be found in all of us.

With a bachelor's in fine arts from the Academy of Art University in San Francisco, Kimberly has been able to adapt her educational background to her life experiences and cultural roots. She has worked on several projects, including book covers, interior illustrations, logo branding, and product packaging.

Website: www.poetagoddess.com
Instagram: @poetagoddess

Become Part
of the Magic

Spirt Bound Press

Website: www.SpiritBoundPress.com
Find us on social media: @SpiritBoundPress